Getting Over Job Search Hurdles

Preparation & Positioning

UNDERSTANDING YOU

First Edition

Copyright © 2013 by Diana Miller, Founder/Director of the Community Job Club, Inc., Expert Career Success Coach and Job Search Strategist.

All rights reserved. No part of this publication may be reproduced, stored in a retrieval system, or transmitted, in photocopying, recording, or otherwise, without written permission from Diana Miller.

This book is dedicated to all the members of the Community Job Club whose determination is to improve their own careers and eagerness, to assist each other in this endeavor, which continues to fuel my passion to serve those dealing with job loss challenges.

ABOUT THE AUTHOR

Diana Miller has a dynamic effect on audiences that few speakers match. Whether she speaks before government agencies, professional job search groups, criminal justice staff, or inmates, Diana delivers her message with impact and style.

A product of many transitions and changes herself; Diana's background makes her a powerful communicator with all groups of people. The depth of her unique ability bridges cultural, racial, educational, and economic gaps. Diana's unique skills allow her to enter situations of conflicting interests and create solutions that lead to success for everyone.

Diana is the Founder/Director of the Community Job Club, Inc., and has been nationally recognized as a job club architect committed to getting job seekers over job search hurdles and helping businesses thrive in challenging times.

She has consulted with government agencies, including the U.S. Department of Labor and the White House Faith Based and Neighborhood Partnership Office, and supported community leaders involved in the establishment of community based job clubs.

As a Career Success Coach and Professional Resume Writer

Diana will help you manage your job search campaign if you are a business executive or someone just starting out to clarify your vision, eliminate roadblocks, and implement action plans that achieve success. This could include interview coaching, career exploration, job search campaign, strategic planning, networking techniques, salary-negotiation strategies, value-based resume writing, and more.

If you are interested in working with Diana you can contact her via email at dmiller@communityjobclub.org or call her at (330) 612-1804. Diana can deliver individualized services via Skype, phone, or in person.

Find Diana on LinkedIn and connect: www.linkedin.com/in/dianamillercj

Table of Contents

PREPARING FOR A SUCCESSFUL JOB SEARCH CAMPAIGN 2
STAGES OF JOB LOSS and JOB LOSS CYCLE 4
COMMON BARRIERS TO JOB SEARCH 7
KNOW YOURSELF 10
CAREER ASSESSMENTS 17
DETERMINE IF A CAREER CHANGE IS RIGHT FOR YOU 26
BECOME SELF-EMPLOYED 28
REVIEWING YOUR ACCOMPLISHMENTS 30
USING YOUR TELEPHONE TO GET A JOB INTERVIEW 42
Write your own… 43
PUTTING IT ALL TOGETHER - SUMMARY OF WHERE YOU ARE RIGHT NOW 44
SETTING GOALS TO REACH THE TARGET 46
YOUR REASON FOR LEAVING YOUR LAST POSITION RESPONSE 48
NETWORK, NETWORK, NETWORK 50
PREPARING A 30-SECOND ELEVATOR PITCH 54
ONE PAGE JOB SEARCH CAMPAIGN MASTER PLAN 57
MAXIMIZING YOUR EXPOSURE TO OPPORTUNITY AND DECISION MAKERS 59
USE OF SOCIAL MEDIA IN JOB SEARCH CAMPAIGNS 59
John T. Doe 64
MARKETING CHANNEL EXPOSURE TECHNIQUE 65
NOW THE FUN PART…WRITING A RESUME THAT GETS INTERVIEWS 67
CREATING COVER LETTERS TO GET INTERVIEWS 78
TIPS FOR SUCCESSFULLY INTERVIEWS 82
SALARY RESEARCH 91
QUICK TIPS FOR NEGOTIATING JOB AND SALARY OFFERS 92
INTERNET CAREER RESOURCES 93
Works Cited 110

PREPARING FOR A SUCCESSFUL JOB SEARCH CAMPAIGN

This book will help you…

- Deal with any emotional, personal or professional challenges related to managing change associated with job loss and career transition.
- Understand your motivation, career strengths, career interests, and values.
- Focus on your uniqueness and its value to you and the marketplace.
- Identify transferable skills and accomplishments.
- Focus on a more realistic future and how to get over the difficult hurdles that may in your way.

The most successful job searches almost always start with a plan. The right amount of preparation, planning, and strategizing is essential.

Planning helps you clarify your goals, understand your skills, target specific jobs/employers, give you more confidence, and puts you a step ahead of competitors. Most of all, it keeps you focused on and in control of your search campaign.

In order to be successful job seekers need to have several things going for them:

1. A organized approach to the task of developing a job search campaign.
2. A profound perception of what value they bring to the table and what they are looking for.
3. A willingness to listen, takes advice, and tries new things.
4. The support of friends, associates, etc. This last item is exceptionally important—This last item is exceptionally important—family support, including your spouse or partner, young children as well as grown kids, parents, in-laws, people you have worked with, etc. Get them involved. Get their ideas and recommendations. Get their help in practice interviews and simulated telephone calls.

I have also found that most unsuccessful job seekers have things in common:

1. Most don't spend a lot of time looking and do not treat the job search as if it were a full time to job to find a job.
2. Most don't use the most effective methods in today's job market.
3. Job seekers often look for any job.
4. They are stuck in their old ways and not open to constructive feedback.

There's no single tool for conducting a successful job search. There are many inventive and efficient ways to go about it. Still, there are some essential tools that all job seekers should comprehend and have in their stash of methods before they start.

Getting Over Job Search Hurdles, Preparation and Positioning, provides the comprehensive insights and realistic advice you need to get over the hurdles and help you plan to launch a successful job search campaign, even in the utmost challenging of times.

So, first things first. Before you get started with your search, you must understand the rules of a successful job search campaign including the Stages of Job Loss and how it can affect your search. Then you can start defining your goals, identifying your accomplishments, develop your plan, and then write your resume and other job search marketing materials.

PRINCIPLES TO LIVE BY DURING A JOB SEARCH CAMPAIGN

Principle 1: If you are unemployed and simply beginning, you should plan on how you spend your cash on hand and follow a budget. Things you can begin doing immediately is to pick espresso at home in place of Starbucks. Put off home remodels, get-a ways, and don't eat out regularly. You may want to address your bank and lenders to check whether you can get some sort of extension or other help. Don't procrastinate, begin right now! Your investment funds can rapidly diminish and your occupation pursuit might take any longer than you suspect.

Principle 2: Only your spouse, companion, mother, maybe sisters and siblings will feel sad for you. So, paying little mind to why you are unemployed, you should encompass yourself with constructive and solid individuals. Feeling sad for yourself and venting is not a productive task, however initiating movement is. Ensure that your loved ones are pumping you up for change and victory.

Principle 3: Wake up and smell the roses. Take a couple of minutes every day and revel in your recently discovered opportunity. When was the last time you didn't need to consider a dead line, a deal, a supervisor, or getting up at 6:00 am? Your cell is very not ringing for the moment and that is fine, for now.

Principle 4: You should conduct your job search as though it was a full time work. Establishing a 6-8 hour a day with activities that will help land your next venture. Do not invest your time pondering or wondering around the house without direction or surfing the web. There is no time to waste. You will work harder at uncovering another venture then you most likely worked in your last effort to find a job. Get up every day, early, get dressed and follow your Master Job Search Campaign Plan.

Principle 5: Accept the actuality of being unemployed. Accept that your pursuit will take more time than you expected. Job seekers frequently underestimate the time it will take and afterward wind up feeling like a flop when they don't obtain employment immediately and get denied after the first interview. There could be loads of meetings, assuming that you are fortunate to get meetings that will wind up not being the employment meant for you to have. Just continue onward, don't surrender. The more no's you get the closer you are to yes.

Principle 6: Avoid disappointment and frustration. If you are requisitioning occupations that you are either over-qualified for or under-qualified for, you are setting yourself up. Don't think because you hold a degree in Mathematics, the nearby supermarket will jump for joy when you stroll in the door and apply you will get hired on the spot.

Principle 7: Accept the adventure of looking for your next opportunity will be stressful. Stress is an ordinary part of the experience and you are not alone, most everyone in transition goes through it. You have to do things that will diminish the anxiety like taking stroll or different sorts of relaxation practices to reduce the stress and tension.

Principle 8: Evaluate and track your progression. At the end of every week, take an inventory of what you achieved throughout the week to get you closer to your objective. Look at what's working and what is not and make essential changes in the plan if things are not working as you had hoped. Along these lines, for instance, assuming that you are getting job notifications from job boards that are not an a good target for what you are looking, then change job notifications until you get better matches.

Principle 9: Reward yourself and don't let your pursuit consume you. Take time at the end of the day following after you have invested your full day of job search and run errands and go for a walk, clean the basement, or have coffee with a job search buddy or close friend who supports your efforts.

STAGES OF JOB LOSS and JOB LOSS CYCLE

Stages of Job Loss Crisis, according to "The Psychology of Termination and Outplacement, by Robert B. Gerber includes: (Gerber)

Stage 1: Shock & or Relief	Stage 7: Panic (degree depends on severance situation)
Stage 2: Denial & Disbelief	Stage 8: Depression
Stage 3: Self-isolation	Stage 9: Understanding & Resignation of the Situation
Stage 4: Anger	Stage 10: Acceptance of Reality
Stage 5: Bargaining	Stage 11: Building a Positive Outlook
Stage 6: Guilt and Remorse	Stage 12: Opportunity, Growth and New Direction

Because each person's reaction to unemployment is unique, there are many similarities that most of job seekers experience. Job Loss Stages include the initial shock, anger and denial phase that come when you face a reality you did not expect (A), where you may not believe that you are really out of a job (particularly if you were fired or let go abruptly), followed by worry, anxiety, and a sense of impending disaster (B) over what you will do next.

After some time, most people begin to "adjust" to the transition and gear up to look for another job. At this point, you may feel hopeful and optimistic about the chances of getting another job. That is the crest of the roller coaster (C).

Depending on the response you get from possible employers, your emotions will vary, alternating between depression, ecstasy, anxiety, and impatience, anger, thankfulness, hopelessness, and irritation (D).

Finally, if the job search is unsuccessful over a long period of time, some people will "burn out" and feel a sense of despair. Sometimes you may even give up the search (H).

Breaking the destructive cycle of unemployment and avoiding burnout is difficult. However, if you allow yourself to be enthusiastic (E), reach out for help and make use of the resources and training programs that are offered to you (F), you may find the next interview lands the job you desire (G) or give up (H).

The transition of unemployment can leave you feeling is out of control and you are a big looser. If you allow yourself to "feel" you will get through it or otherwise the pain, like cancer, repressed emotions slowly and steadily kill from the inside.

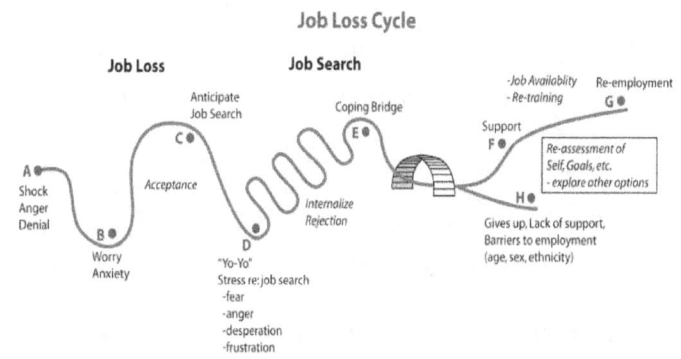

The shock of the termination can create reactions that employees may exhibit such as: (Gerber)

<u>Victims:</u> Victims immerse themselves in self-pity and despair. Their visions of a dismal future often become self –fulfilled prophesy. They either express hostility or become frightened and depressed. Victims frequently become sick. Almost everyone who is laid off will initially spend some time feeling like a victim.

<u>Survivors:</u> The survivor role may emerge after the initial shock of layoff passes. Instead of feeling sorry for themselves, survivors fight. The fighting spirit is healthier than the weariness of sufferers. However, the survivor is high-anxiety, eventually resulting in burnout.

<u>Navigators:</u> Navigators handle the shock of a layoff the best. They recognize their pain, let go of the past quickly, and get on with their lives. This attitude allows them to see the opportunities that are created as a result of a dramatic change. Navigators create the future they want, sometimes fulfilling lifelong dreams.
Navigators:

1. It's time to forget about the past and take responsibility for your own security so put yourself in good hands...your own.

2. Manage the stress of change imposed by others by creating some change of your own. It's up to you to devise exciting new plans that do involve you.
3. Life is difficult, but misery is optional. Making the best of a bad situation is good advice.

So, bottom line, you MUST monitor your feelings and thoughts and be very aware of your "negative self-talk". You cannot think about the "should ofs" or would ofs" of the "if only I had of, etc." You have to not "should of yourself". This type of thinking will continue to create mixed emotions and lead to negative results.

Get busy and get out there. Some ideas to get started.

Job Club Support Groups: There are tons of job clubs and programs throughout the country. Job Clubs can help you maintain your sanity and teach you the most up-to-date job-hunting skills. Such groups are available through local employment centers, employment agencies, colleges, universities, and social service agencies. Visit the Department of Labor to find a job club near you. www.dol.gov/jobclubs

Set Immediate Goals: Creating a plan by establishing an outline of specific activities you need to do that includes deadlines for completion will help you feel successful. But remember to keep you goals realistic and practical. Otherwise you are setting yourself up for failure.

Get Some Retraining: Listing your skills and reviewing your strengths is very significant in identifying the kinds of jobs that you can do and the kind of training you may need to consider, in order, to remain competitive.

Develop you list of Personal Contacts: Your network of contacts is essential so staying in touch is a critical piece of surviving the search. Going to interviews for information on companies will keep you in tune with possible openings within various companies--many of which are never advertised.

Take Bridge /Temp Job: This may help you pay the bills and keep you your head above water while you continue to look for something more substantial.

Do Volunteer Work: Volunteer work is a wonderful way to learn new skills, offer your talents, and improve your self-esteem. When you volunteer, you make contacts and see new possibilities.

Do the Little Things: Do all the things that you have been saving for a dreary day--it gives you a sense of accomplishment.

Remember… Job Seekers who are looking for work and treat it like a full time job are usually first to land their next opportunity.

COMMON BARRIERS TO JOB SEARCH

At any given minute in your pursuit, it is possible to blame others or come up with all kind of excuses at to why you are not arriving at what you need when you need it. Typically the main reason people are not successful in reaching their goals, is "they get in their own way".

The real hindrances are inner remnants of doubting fears and rigidity to change. In other words, the normal, everyday psychological baggage that goes a long with the process of change that everyone experiences a long the way. The best way to manage such limitations is first to recognize them openly, and after that decided rather or not you are ready to take the steps vital to overcome them.

1. What are the biggest internal hurdles getting in the way of your job search?

_____

_____

2. What is the single most prevailing personal hurdle or behavior that might stand in the way of you doing what it takes to find a job with full job happiness?

_____

_____

3. What steps can you take right now to overcome the hurdles you listed above?

_____

_____

_____

_____

WHERE YOU ARE RIGHT NOW & DO YOU NEED TO GET FOCUSED

A productive job search campaign comes right down to only one thing: keeping it straightforward. By streamlining the job search methods you use, it's easier to recognize success and you are less likely to not get overwhelmed. Most job seekers have issue getting started because they are clueless of where to begin. Instead of being focused on only one important part of the process at a time, they attempt to try and do several things at the same time and when the results don't come fast enough, they give up.

Think of your job search as a series of hurdles that once properly cleared can yield glorious results. It's simply a matter of separating the central components into manageable parts, making it easier for you to realize success throughout every stage of your search.

By devoting time and energy at the start of your search and excluding jobs that aren't a decent fit for you, you will truly pay less time on your job search campaign and have success faster than you may think. Sort of like carpenter's advice: "measure twice, cut once". It's that easy.

Before you start, you need to find out how ready you are right at this minute to before you leap in with both feet. By identifying areas you may need to improve to achieve success will help you with setting your goals and get better organized.

Take a moment to answer each of the following questions "Yes" or "No", and then total your answers at the end of each section to determine your level of preparation. If you are not as prepared as you thought you were, then now is the time to get prepared or you will be wasting a lot of time.

Self-Awareness

What you know about yourself and your work preferences

_____ Are your career goals clear and can you describe them to others?

_____ Do you know what activities you do best and enjoy most in a job?

_____ Can you list at least five skills and abilities you have which you can use in your next position?

_____ Do you know what work environment you prefer and why?

_____ If the position will require travel are you open to that?

_____ How do you like to be supervised and how much responsibility do you want in your next position?

_____ Can you summarize your professional experience in terms of your value, experience and achievements?

A score of less than six "Yes" answers indicates the need to examine your work preferences more closely before proceeding with your job search.

Job Search Campaign

What do you know about conducting a successful job search campaign

_____ Do you have at least 1 targeted position for your job search?

_____ Have you considered what your geographic areas of preferences are and or identified your limitations?

_____ Can you name at least three resources that list job openings and are in your targeted area of interest?

_____ Do you have a list of at least 3 sources that could help you identify potential employers?

_____ Do you know how to find employers that are interviewing right now for your targeted position?

_____ Have you talked to professionals and others associated with your targeted position?

_____ Do you have a list of employers that interest you and are within your geographical area?

A score of less than five "Yes" answers indicates the need to learn more about effective job search strategies.

The gaps between where you are today and where you would like to be as a high performing, active, effective job seeker clearly shows which areas need your closest attention.

KNOW YOURSELF

Obviously, you don't want just any job and you don't want to waste a lot of time. If you define your goals and objectives now, rather targeting whatever comes along, this will allow you to find what you are truly meant to be doing. You may need income right now, even if you consider your next job as a means to an end, make sure it fits into the big picture.

It's unproductive not to have a specific job target when you are looking for your next opportunity. Consider the following situation.

1. **Two people are looking for work**. One **says she is open to "anything** that comes along" and sends resumes for almost every job that appears in the employment classifieds week after week. Even though she gets a lot of rejections, she also gets invited to quite a few interviews. The jobs that she is applying for are ones that neither suit nor interest her. In her mind she is thinking that she has accomplished a lot and is ready to follow the same method the next week.

2. The **second job seeker follows a different tactic**. She **targets three specific jobs** that she knows she can do well and wants to do. She researches tons employers in her area who can use people for those jobs, narrows her list of those companies she really would like to work for and focuses her efforts on contacting those employers directly. She does not get invited in for a lot of interviews, but she does have a few quality discussions with prospective employers that lead to two job offers.

Working laboriously to flush out every job lead is not always the best strategy. A better approach is to target the jobs that will bring you satisfaction and also take advantage of your most significant skills and abilities. By focusing your efforts, you will make the best use of your time and, amazingly, increase your chances of finding meaningful employment rapidly.

A good job target is a work direction that combines your personal interests with your natural talents and skills.

The first hurdle in organizing a job search campaign involves gathering information about you to assist making a decision about a position that fits you like a glove. This focus will help you narrow your options and target suitable employers and cut out wasted time.

Every one of us has our own individual or unique set of skills, natural talents, and desires. Identifying skills and talents is vital to your success. A skill is something you've learned to do. A natural talent is something you've been born with or, at least, seem naturally qualified to do. It's important to recognize the difference between the two.

Being skilled at something and doing it are two different things because you still might not find it interesting. Chances are, however, if you are inherently talented at something; there will usually be a related link between that particular talent and your interests. Put another way: you are more apt to enjoy doing what comes effortlessly than what you have simply been taught to do.

When your work is not a good fit with who you are, it creates stress and frustration. If your work isn't fulfilling and doesn't come natural it will become frustrating, boring, and you won't want to get up and go in the morning. If you can imagine working in a position that requires you to write print ads all day (a somewhat solitary and boring task that calls for accuracy and makes sense) when your passion that really invigorates you is to be in a creative setting, conceptualizing and developing marketing ideas.

It is clear that when your work is in alignment with your natural talents and passions, there is harmony and your feel satisfied. Instead of being a basketball player when you cannot make a basket you play baseball because you can hit grand slams every time you get the bat in your hands because it comes natural to you and brings you great satisfaction.

Doing the exercises in the book will help you shape up your search and avoid jumping at opportunities that are not satisfying or even good fits. Invest the time now to get your job search campaign in tiptop form to find your ideal job choice. Skipping this process is like losing tennis match you play because you are really passionate about being a baseball player but haven't pursued the game.

These exercises will help you do the following:

- Make strategic choices to act offensively rather than defensively in your job search campaign.
- Leverage your time by pursuing the "right fit" and opportunities.
- Impress interviewers by knowing what you want. Gain confidence-targeting positions where you can be a career champion and have a competitive edge over others who are competing for the same positions. Then you can develop a solid Job Search Master Plan that will help you stay on track.

The principal elements of the Job Search Campaign Master Plan is to identify your:

1. **Functions:** represents job tiles and tasks.
2. **Industries:** refers to where you will apply your functional skills.
3. **Happiness:** is synonymous with purpose and something that makes you want to get up and go to work each day.
4. **Individuality**: refers to how you see yourself – your internal self-image.
5. **What's most important**: things that matter to you personally that you want in your next job.
6. **Natural talents**: refer to your personality and what comes natural.

If you can answer the question shat do you really want to do when you grow up thoroughly and honestly, you will save yourself a lot of time and might even land a job you actually love?

Other questions to think about are:

- Do work for someone else or be your own boss?

- Is a steady paycheck important or do you love the possibility of making more through commissions?

- Are you interested in a low-pressure position that is less stressful or do you want to be the leader?

- Deciding what you really want in your next opportunity is your first step toward landing your ideal job.

THE HUNT FOR HAPPINESS

Define Your Function, what makes YOU Happy, & Find Your Purpose

This step will transform your work from — paycheck, to — passion as you write a statement describing your passion, what makes you happy and your plan for your dream job. Purpose and poverty don't need to be one of the same. If the only reason behind your work is a paycheck I am confident that there can be much more. Earning an attractive income is perfectly fine, if that is significant to you. The best way to focus your search is to pair your natural talents, passion and purpose with market demand.

Being able to discover your true passion by enhancing your self-perception will give you genuine and sustained happiness at work if you follow your plan.

The Happiness at Work Formula: Happiness Work = E + R + C, developed by Peter Weddle, the author and editor of more than two dozen books, including "The Career Activist Republic, Work Strong: Your Personal Career Fitness System," and Weddle's 2011/12 Guide to Employment Sites on the Internet. (Weddle)

E = Engagement or what naturally fascinates you and challenges you.

R = Relevance or what naturally seems worthwhile and important to you.

C = Choice or what you naturally focus on and decide to do when you give yourself permission to do so.

JOB SATISFACTION

Every job you've got ever had some duties you enjoyed and a few you despised. Not to surprising that, individuals tend to perform more efficiently when their work tasks and responsibilities correspond with their career interests and natural abilities. How much satisfaction you derive from work is directly connected to the match between your personal career interests and the scope of a particular job.

Think about what you enjoy doing, what is necessary to you, and what you are doing well.

Ask yourself these questions:

- What activities bring you satisfaction?
- What projects do others invite you to perform?
- Were you ever accredited, presented with an award, or complimented for one thing you did extraordinarily well?

- What skills and talents have you ever used in the past to reach your goals?
- Were you ever told you are doing things far better than others?
- Think about a time when you felt prosperous. What were you doing?
- What motivates you to leap out of bed in the morning - raring to go?
- Was there ever a time that you only achieved results that exceeded other's expectations?
- What is one thing you did that left you feeling proud?

Understanding the value of the strengths and accomplishments you've gained, gives you a foothold throughout interviews by being able to answer the question, "Why should I hire you?

Need options? The most extensive list of position titles and functional areas is housed in the Occupational Outlook Handbook at the U.S. Governments Labor Statistics page online (the book is also available in print at libraries & bookstores).

DO YOU FIT INTO THE COMPANY CULTURE?

Knowing your personal values is vital when you are in transition and looking for you next opportunity. Employees who believe in and support the goals of their employers and usually repeat the interests and personalities of their coworkers' are more likely to achieve success over those whose values conflict with others within the company.

Ponder the following questions.

1) Is your work rewarding and does it include use of your natural skills and aptitudes?
2) Do you add to the success of the organization when you are working?
3) Does management acknowledge your contributions by pay increases or awards?
4) Are you acquiring and developing new skills that are in line with what you want to next?
5) Are you at the top of you're game or is there room for advancement in your career?
6) Does your current job or previous position suit your long-term goals?

Do You Have What It Takes to be Successful?

- What is your definition of success?
- Is being successful what makes you happy?
- Do success and satisfaction go hand in hand or do you think they are different?

- Does having a lot success mean you make a lot of money?
- Do you know what kind of career would make you happy? If yes, what are you doing now to prepare yourself? How committed are you to achieving your own career happiness?

Imagine Having the Ideal Job You Have Always Dreamed of.

- What type of job would it be and exactly what would you be doing?
- What kind of people would you want to work with and how many?
- Where would it be located?
- How would you spend each day?

What if you just inherited a lot of money from an aunt that you didn't even know you had. All the pressure would be off and actually you would be in a place where don't need to work ever again. Unfortunately though, your aunt threw some glitches into the mix. She gave the money to some investment bankers who will only give the money to you after you have met certain conditions.

First condition: For the first three years, you will be given $50,000 for annual expenses. You can do whatever you choose, but you must spend time learning about something that really interests you. How would you spend your time and what sort of things would you be doing?

Second Condition: After the first 3 years, your aunt requires you to spend half of the inheritance on a project that will improve the lives of others. What would that be?

A lot of food for thought, right????

Complete the Career Assessment: "Getting to Know Yourself and Where You are RIGHT NOW"

This will give you a good inventory of

- Common concerns
- Personal concerns
- Positive factors about your strengths

This is a critical step. If you do not know your marketable skills, it will be much harder to prepare your marketing materials, such as a resume and other materials that you will need to get over the unemployment hurdle and land a position in where you are a good fit.

CAREER ASSESSMENTS
GETTING TO KNOW YOURSELF AND WHERE YOU ARE RIGHT NOW.

Listed below are many common concerns that can become hurdles in any job campaign.

	Lack of industry experience		Experience is limited to just one industry
	Unemployed		Necessary to transfer to a new industry
	Short period of employment		Took early retirement
	Appears to be a "job hopper"		Afraid to move from long term employment
	Education is limited		Always lateral moves...NO PROMOTIONS
	Present income is low		Can be too old
	Education is not related to career		Present industry is not a growth industry
	Can be too young		Academic background is mediocre
	Transition from military to industry		Specialist in one field
	Re-entry to the workplace		Experience has been in structured corporations
	Salary is too high		Experience has been in small companies
	Management experience is missing		Promotions lacking
	Passed over for promotion		Generalist in many fields
	Salary history is low		Line experience only NOT STAFF
	Need additional experience in Senior Management		Need additional experience in Management/Supervision
	Staff experience only, not line		Need additional experience in Financial Management

PERSONAL CONCERNS

Too passive	Too arrogant	Poor communicator
Not realistic	Very nervous	Minimum interpersonal ability
Foreign birth	Foreign education	Not a citizen of U.S.A

Additional concerns of your own

_____
_____
_____
_____
_____
_____
_____
_____
_____
_____
_____
_____
_____
_____
_____
_____
_____

POSITIVES FACTORS...NOW IS YOUR CHANCE TO RELATE ALL THE POSITIVE FACTORS ABOUT YOUR CAREER STRENGTHS AS WELL AS THE PERSONAL QUALITIES, WHICH ARE IMPORTANT TO A NEW EMPLOYER.

CHECK THE POSITIVE.

Professional responsibilities	College degrees	Superior interpersonal skills
Proven manager	Expert communicator	Leadership
A decision maker	Fine "track record"	Have definite goals
High drive for success	Good common sense	Self-confident
Strong analytical ability	Can solve problems	Seasoned executive
Reorganized/revitalized	Multi-plant background	People oriented
Heavy business contacts	International experience	Conscientious
Fluent in languages	Get the job done (on time)	Diplomatic
Can work independently	Superb teacher and trainer	Honest
High ethics and character	Inspire others	Resourceful
Calm under pressure	Management expert	Administrative skills
Strong team player	Conceptualizes	Very determined

MARKETABLE SKILLS: REVIEW THE FOLLOWING SKILLS AND CHECK ALL THAT YOU FEEL ARE CORRECT STATEMENTS ABOUT YOURSELF. NEXT, REVIEW THE CHECKED SKILLS AND HIGHLIGHT THE 10 SKILLS THAT HAVE THE GREATEST PRIORITY FOR YOU.

Analyze data	Distribution	Own/operate business
Anticipate problem	Demonstrate/present	Organize people
Assess situations	Delegate	Organize tasks
Advise people	Edit	Organize data

Arbitrate	Educate	Organize equipment
Arrange functions	Engineer	Policy making
Audit records	Estimate	Production
Budget money	Establish	Persuade others
Buy products/service	Execute	Public relations
Control people	Expedite	Precision work
Control situation	Follow through	Research
Control costs	Guide/lead	Rehabilitate people
Coordinate activities	Generate information	Recruit people
Create	Gather information	Sell
Classify information	Handle complaints	Supervise
Calculate numbers	Help people	Service customers
Correspond w/others	Inspect products	Speak in public
Compile statistics	Interview people	Schedule
Construct buildings	Investigate	Set up systems
Check for accuracy	Implement procedures	Set up equipment
Converse w/others	Inventory	Set goals/objectives
Consult w/others	Instruct	Train/develop
Contact w/others	Initiate actions	Trouble shoot
Conceptualize ideas	Interpret data	Verify
Cope w/deadlines	Improvise	Write procedures
Chart information	Illustrate	Write reports
Contract with others	Listen	Write promo material

Conduct	Liaise	Write proposals
Compute data	Manage people	Write technical work
Compare data	Monitor progress	
Decision making	Manage a business	
Motivate others	Negotiate	

PERSONALITY TRAIT: REVIEW THE FOLLOWING SKILLS AND CHECK ALL THAT YOU FEEL ARE CORRECT STATEMENTS ABOUT YOURSELF. NEXT, REVIEW THE CHECKED SKILLS AND HIGHLIGHT OR BOLD THE 10 SKILLS THAT HAVE THE GREATEST PRIORITY FOR YOU.

Academic	Accurate	Versatile
Aggressive	Ambitious	Adaptable
Assertive	Broadminded	Artistic
Businesslike	Clear-thinking	Competent
Competitive	Confident	Conscientious
Conservative	Considerate	Cooperative
Courageous	Creative	Curious
Deliberate	Democratic	Dependable
Determined	Dignified	Discreet
Dominant	Eager	Efficient
Emotional	Energetic	Enterprising
Enthusiastic	Fair-minded	Farsighted
Firm	Flexible	Forceful
Friendly	Helpful	Honest
Humorous	Idealistic	Imaginative
Independent	Ingenious	Intellectual
Intelligent	Inventive	Logical
Loyal	Mature	Methodical
Meticulous	Open-minded	Opportunistic

Optimistic	Organized	Outgoing
Patient	Poised	Polite
Practical	Precise	Progressive
Punctual	Productive	Quiet
Rational	Realistic	Reasonable
Reliable	Serious	Self-confident
Sensible	Spontaneous	Sincere
Sociable	Teachable	Stable
Tactful	Tolerant	Tenacious
Thorough	Understanding	Trustworthy

JOB SATISFACTION FACTORS: EVALUATE EACH OF THE FOLLOWING JOB SATISFACTION STATEMENTS AND RANK THE TOP STATEMENTS IN ORDER OF PRIORITY; 1 BEING THE STATEMENT OF GREATEST PRIORITY; 15 THE LEAST.

	Use of your problem-solving ability		Hands on implementation
	Instructing other people? Training		Need to be stretched? Challenged
	Doing precise or detailed work		Being able to see results from your work
	Being creative		Making decisions and using your own initiative
	Working as part of a team		Influencing or persuading other people
	Making group presentation		Being competitive on the job
	Helping society and other people		Working under deadline pressure
	Having authority and responsibilities		Having a variety in your tasks and duties

	Working at a quick pace		Having stability and security in the job
	Being independent /setting own schedule		Earning recognition / being a leader in you
	Being considered the expert		Earning large sums of money
	Traveling		Working outside the office environment
	Working indoors in a specific work area		Having varied work environments
	Professional affiliations		Delegating

TOP MARKETABLE SKILLS & PERSONALITY TRAITS YOU WOULD LIKE TO USE ON YOUR NEXT JOB

	Marketable Skills		Personality Traits
1		1	
2		2	
3		3	
4		4	
5		5	
6		6	
7		7	
8		8	
9		9	
10		10	

List all the things that you liked in your previous job (rank them in order of preference):

List all the things you did not like in your previous job and want to avoid in your next (rank them in order of maximum dislike):

	Liked		Disliked

LIST ALL THE THINGS THAT YOU WOULD LIKE TO BE INCLUDED IN YOUR IDEAL JOB (RANK THEM IN ORDER OF IMPORTANCE):

WORK ENVIRONMENT:

WRITE OUT WHAT YOU WOULD LIKE TO SEE IN THE IDEAL WORK ENVIRONMENT AND ALSO WHAT YOU DON'T WANT TO SEE – WHAT WOULD DETRACT FOR THE "IDEAL." THIS WILL HELP YOU EVALUATE POTENTIAL JOBS IN TERMS OF PERSONAL PREFERENCE. FOR EXAMPLE, IF YOU PREFER A LARGE COMPANY WITH A STRUCTURED WORK ENVIRONMENT, THIS IS IMPORTANT TO NOTE. IT WILL HELP YOU SINGLE OUT SPECIFIC COMPANIES FOR YOUR TARGET LIST.

Use the terms below to describe your ideal work environment: Sample Listing of Favorable Work Attribute

The Company	The Job
Consistent growth	Good salary
Challenging environment	Independence
Internal promotion opportunities	Defined authority
Sound structure and policies	Defined responsibility
Team spirit	Good interpersonal relations
Motivation	Chance to be creative
Excellent products and services	Clearly defined duties
Educational opportunities	Effective communication
Reputation for honesty and fair play	Opportunity to learn
Good surroundings	Travel
Modern facilities	Opportunity for promotion

Good benefits	Challenging work
Good location	Interesting fellow employees
Well-established management	Chance to build a team
Security	Adequate time to do a good job
Modern management	OTHERS?
Genuine interest in everyone's advancement	
Management responsive to individual policies problems	

My ideal work environment would be

_____
_____
_____
_____
_____
_____
_____
_____
_____

What are your top 3 functions you see yourself doing in your next position?

Write your fulfillment statement that describes how your functions, happiness, passion and your purpose will fit into your next ideal work environment and position.

_____

_____

_____

_____

_____

_____

_____

_____

DETERMINE IF A CAREER CHANGE IS RIGHT FOR YOU

Before you change careers, some serious soul searching is in order. You have to think about what you like or don't like about what you did in your previous position or what you are doing in your current one. For instance, if your biggest downside at your current place of work is hit or miss boss, maybe the solution is a new job within the same field rather than a total career makeover.

Remember: Don't dismiss a career change only because of your age. A younger person may feel he or she ought to spend several years within the same profession before creating a change. An older person may not want to take the risk of what a career change may require. What's necessary, however, is whether or not your profession is creating the satisfaction and the best use of your talents.

Figure out that Career you want

If you recognize you don't just like the career you have but you aren't sure what to do next, create an inventory of the type of positions that makes you happy and fulfills you goals. Next, take that list to your friends and family. Sometimes, an outside perspective can yield insights you never expected.

Visit the CareerOneStop, sponsored by the U. S. Department of Labor, Employment and Training Administration and explore additional resources to help you figure out what career path to pursue:

- The Skills Profiler identifies skills and matches them to jobs.
- O*NET's Ability Profiler matches strengths with occupations.
- O*NET's Interest Profiler identifies broad interest areas.
- O*NET's Work Importance Locator identifies job features that are relevant to you.
- Employability Checkup provides a snapshot of your employability.
- myPathway
- www.careerpath.com
- www.todaysmilitary.com/before-serving/asvab-test

CareerOneStop is...

- Your source for employment information and inspiration
- The place to manage your career
- Your pathway to career success
- Tools to help job seekers, students, businesses and career professionals

Notes:

BECOME SELF-EMPLOYED

The world of work is changing rapidly due to globalization and technology and the changes are leaving a lot people in the dust. It is up to you to make sure you familiarize yourself with at least the basics of technology and learn how to maneuver the Internet. With a laptop, an Internet connection, and a few clicks of a button, you'll be able to begin a business in the spur-of-the-moment and all on-line. The key here is to find a customer, a solution, and the simplest way to in get paid

Here are some things to considering exploring if you are thinking about creating your business.

Find people, in your industry, who work freelance or as consultants. Talk to them and find out how they do it, what they've learned, and what the problems and drawbacks are. Recap your findings below.

1. Reasons for consider being self-employed:

_____
_____
_____
_____

2. What they enjoy about being self-employed:

_____
_____
_____
_____

3. What they dislike about being self-employed:

_____
_____
_____
_____

4. Downside of being self-employed and ways to over come them.

_____
_____
_____
_____

Examine your most recent job, making a list of what responsibilities need to be done at the employer's location and what could be done away from the employer's location.

Employer's location:

_____
_____
_____
_____
_____

Away from the location:

_____
_____
_____
_____
_____

Go to the library and read current publications concerned with organizing a home office, starting your own business, and so on. Write a short composition entitled either *Why I May Start My Own Business* or *Why I Don't Want to be Self-Employed*.

REVIEWING YOUR ACCOMPLISHMENTS

By taking a close look at your life and career achievements, you can begin to formulate activities and jobs you might want to do in your future. Knowing and expressing what you do well will help you:

- Build self-confidence, a key to success
- Locate the position that fits you best
- Develop your resume and other job search marketing materials that you need for success
- Communicate effectively in interviews and meetings

An accomplishment is an activity that gives you pleasure, fulfillment and a feeling of pride and success. It can be large or small in scope; it can be routine or extraordinary; frequent or only once, work related or personal. **The key is how you felt about it -- not how others judged it.** These accomplishments represent you functioning at your best, sometimes overcoming difficulties, and believing in yourself and your ideas. While you may understand the necessity of this exercise, you may also be feeling somewhat uncomfortable with it. The following addresses these barriers:

Seven Common Barriers to "Blowing Your Own Horn"

1) You've been taught that nice people don't.
2) You don't want to be seen as "hogging credit"… "I truly did not do it alone – others helped."
3) You feel that your business is no one's concern but yours… "I know that I am capable, so why should I have to convince others?"
4) You have not had to do it very often.
5) You don't take credit for the many things you have really accomplished… "It's all in a day's work"…"It is just my job."
6) You are not sure how to do it without sounding egotistical.

There is a great deal of difference between empty bragging and the confidence that comes from knowing your skills and being optimistic about your future. After reviewing your accomplishments you will probably feel a natural sense of your own worth and have a positive outlook toward your ability to contribute in the future.

A Checklist To Jog Your Memory About Your Accomplishments

Have you:

1) Accomplished more with the same/fewer resources? (How? Results?)

- Rebuilt menu, budget, team and kitchen to prepare and sell food for a 3-day event with over 100,000 attendees. We were able to serve over 13,000 customers in 3 days and broke records for volume and revenue.
- Was given the project to engineer a 26-mile fiber optic ring. Did the entire survey, pole attachments, make-ready, etc… myself. Usually a team of people is required to do this.
- Worked on facility projects in 9 cities with a team of 2 people.
- Took over a project from a large telecom provider in which they were using a team of people and had been working over a year to identify, negotiate and procure sites in which to relocate telecom equipment. I took over the project re-engineered the type of facility in which to procure, devised a leasing structure to fix and contain overall cost, did a site search in 4 cities, implemented the plan and in 3 months was able to secure half of the 36 sites needed for the project and identify locations for the remaining sites. (all under budget)
- Once the previous project was in hand, I was put on a project to build an entire dispatch department to service over 200 technician's that were over 1,000 miles away. Developed and used one of the 1st text messaging systems for getting work to the field for installation and service.
- Built a measuring matrix for call center call flow and scheduling for a 24/7 inbound call center.
- Created "Colorado Dog Biscuit" an all-natural dog biscuit company with 7 varieties. Recipes, product names, graphic design, testing, packaging, marketing, sales, baking/production (maxed at 500 lbs. per week), events, accounting, distribution, web site.
- Created "Allentown Stained Glass" a custom stained glass window manufacturer. Design, marketing, sales, manufacturing, installation, accounting. (13 yrs., over 2,200 windows, doors, lamps)
- Designed and Self-constructed two single family homes of over 3,000 sq. ft. (carpentry, electrical, drywall, insulation, cabinetry, tile, trim, paint, stone masonry, concrete flatwork, landscaping, windows and doors)
- Devised routing methodology for servicing over 110,000 customer homes in a 3-month period, which resulted in hitting full year productivity and sales metrics.
- Built measuring models in Excel for determining customer flow, worker productivity vs. revenue and several other metrics, which allowed for revamping of work scheduling.

- Creative sourcing for countless materials, fleet vehicles, office supplies, office furniture, facilities, construction materials, etc...
- Started an operation with an office trailer in a parking lot of a facility that was being constructed and built the entire operation in 3 months. Complete with 3 grade levels of technical staff (fully trained), warehouse (fully stocked), fleet of vehicles (fully outfitted), necessary tools, administrative staff and budgets.
- Devised and created an entirely new model for building operational facilities in the cable TV industry. Utilized out-of-business car dealerships which had almost every aspect of fit-out needed to successfully built Ops facilities. High traffic visibility, double-parking, parts department for warehousing, part disbursement and electronics repair. Technical equipment installation in auto repair area, administrative area, customer service/payment center, marketing and sales, lot storage.
- In my career/life I have consistently come up with creative solutions to complicated issues, completed projects in time, under budget and exceeded expectations.

2. Received awards(s), special recognition, etc. (What? Why?)
    - My recognition came in the form of progression through the industry ranks. Cable TV installer, shop steward, supervisor, manager, director, general manager, vice president, and entrepreneur.
3. Increased efficiency? (How? Results?)
    - See above.
4. Solved difficult problem(s) (How? Results?)
    - See above
5. Accomplished something for the first time? (What? Result?)
    - See above
6. Developed, created, designed or invented something? (What? Why important?)
    - See above
7. Prepared original papers, reports, articles? (What? Why important?)
    - See above
    - Macro-economic financial forecasting, trading model methodologies and general financial observations. (Daily newsletter, wrote papers on certain topics, gave presentations)
    - In addition, I built budgets and a multiple city rollout plan for operations in Boston, MA. I did it in both spreadsheet and visual form. Included every detail from staff, fleet, facilities, warehousing, technical equipment, customer service, office equipment, etc....
8. Managed work group, department? (Who? How many? Results?)
    - Managed in-house and contract installation, Ops, construction, call center, design, administrative, production staffs of as little 2 and as many as 200.
9. Saved the company money? (How? How much?)

- See above. One project in particular…Due to the team completing in time and under budget resulted in a $2M bonus for the company.

10. Supervised, managed or trained employees? (Where? How many? Results?)
    - See above

11. Increased sales? (How? By how much?)
    - The recipe…..Conduct overall business management due diligence, create production and customer service metrics, measure and allocate resources. Begin to view results and adjust where necessary.

12. Been promoted or upgraded? (When? Why important?)
    - See above.

13. Increased production? (How? Results?)
    - A couple of more examples…..Increased installer productivity by 20% after creating routing methodology (pre computer software)
    - Devised new way to submit permits and creating relationships with to utility companies allowed for a large increase in turnaround.
    - Pre-prepping certain menu items and transporting them prior to an event.
    - Looking at how any process or operation conducts its business and then creating a unique model for analyzing that business usually leads to the best results in increasing productivity.
    - All of these items not only increased productivity but created substantial cost savings in several areas.

14. Identified problem(s) others did not see? (What? Results?)
    - See above.

15. Developed or implemented a new system or procedure? (What? Benefit?)
    - See above.
    - New systems and procedures constantly evolved and were implemented as computers and software became a bigger and bigger part of any business.
    - The revolution in telecom over my 20+-year career made change "the norm". There were new systems and procedures on a weekly basis as the technology and end product evolved from a basic 12 channel cable TV system, through the microwave age, the invention and changes in set top boxes (my employer was a pioneer in this), integration of computer technology, the introduction of fiber optics, the birth of the digital age and the internet.

16. Reduced downtime? (How? How much? Result?)

17. Established safety record? (What? Result?)

18. Managed budget? (How much? Result?)
    - I have built and managed budgets up to and exceeding $10M.

19. Repaired equipment? (Which? Result?)
    - Facilities, vehicles, electronics, computers.

20.   Met company standards under unusual/difficult circumstances (What? How?)
- Unusual and difficult were usually the norm. Especially, in the start-up environment.
- Personal philosophy…."Do what you say you are going to do!" This is the basis of measurement for any employee/company.
- # of installs
- # of homes passed with serviceable network.
- # of customer service calls taken
- Emergency call-outs due to weather, cable cuts, accidents
1. Budgets met
2. Timelines met
3. Quality standards met
4. Construction deadlines
5. Product freshness.
6. Trading success, research confirmed.
7. Teams built and working with other aspects of the business

Following are some specific ways documenting accomplishments will move the action forward in your Job Search Campaign Master Plan . . .

JOB SELECTION - Accomplishments identify skills and experiences, which support your chosen career opportunities.

SALARY NEGOTIATION - Accomplishments tell an employer of your potential value. At the time of salary negotiation, accomplishments support your perceived worth.

TASK-SPECIFIC RESPONSE - Accomplishments allow you to respond to task-specific requirements with well-worded, results-oriented information.

KEY TALENT (QUALIFICATIONS FOR THE JOB) SUPPORT - It is one thing to say "excellent communication skills," but supporting the claimed talent with an accomplishment solidifies the claim by providing proof.

ALLOWS THE LISTENER TO DETERMINE VALUE OF YOUR EFFORTS - Each person values his/her accomplishments (as well as those of others) on a personal scale. This scale places more importance on some and less on others. In unstructured conversations, the mismatch between your values of various skills and the interviewers can detract from the progress of the interview.

Because the accomplishment format is consistent, the interviewer is allowed to manage the conversation about your experience according to their scale of importance, not necessarily yours.

And, since the interviewer retains the posture of being in charge, a feeling of "agreement of importance" is established between you as the candidate and the interviewer. This kind of agreement makes a you appear competent, likable, and a good fit . . . eminently capable without being pushy or overbearing.

This is vital in job search success and significantly reduces the possibility of being "threatening" to the interviewer.

PROVIDES A FORUM FOR JOB-RELATED DISCUSSION - Because a well-formed accomplishment does not tell the whole story, it will often urge the interviewer/reader to want more information. "How did you do that?" is a frequently heard question, in relation to an accomplishment.

(This is an excellent opportunity for a turn-around question. "There are three issues identified in that Accomplishment - What was done, how it was done, and the result . . . which aspect are you most interested in?" A question may be raised, "Is this indicative of the challenges I'll be facing here?" In each case, the use of your accomplishments as a guide for the interview provides you with a perfect platform for enriching the conversation and probing the opportunities for employment at the organization.)

FOLLOW-UP - When following up on an interview, a network meeting, a chance meeting, or any other contact, if a specific accomplishment was discussed, or if specific talents and skills were identified, a properly formatted selection of your accomplishments becomes an ideal element of ongoing communication.

An important note: During a phone interview, keep a printed list of accomplishments handy. Obviously, when reciting them verbally, you will do so in a grammatically appropriate manner.

Accomplishment List

Reviewing what you have done in your life, please briefly describe eight contributions or achievements -- at least six should be from your work experience.

1.	
2.	
3.	
4.	
5.	
6.	
7.	
8.	

Next, Describe Your Accomplishments

For each accomplishment, describe the challenge, what you did, how you did it, and the results you obtained. If you were part of a group focus on your role in the group. As a result you will be able to better discuss your accomplishments in the interview.

Challenge:

What you needed to do, why you needed to do it, and the type of difficulties you confronted.

Actions:

What you did --- use active verbs (such as "saved", or "redirected").

Results

What you obtained – use quantifiable or measurable terms (e.g., dollars saved or earned, percentage improvement, or decrease, numbers involved, etc.). Even if figures are not applicable in some instances, describe the results in tangible or measurable term

Example 1

Short Title:	Contract Negotiations

Date and Place:	1996 - Sun Bright Corporation

Challenge: At a time when the company was losing money, it was involved in negotiations with two unions. It badly needed some concessions from the unions. As chief labor negotiator, I needed to develop a bargaining strategy that would enable us to reduce labor costs.

Actions: Surveyed common practices with regard to compensation and benefit levels in the industry. Studied concession bargaining strategies, activities and outcomes. Developed a negotiating strategy based on ranking needed concessions and establishing priorities.

Results: *Reduced labor 30% through contract negotiations*

Example 2

Short Title:	Automated Office Operations

Date and Place: 1997, Western Corporation

Challenge: Within two months, needed to automate department operations to respond to a large increase in business. Also, the department had to maintain its productivity standards.

Actions: Researched possible software packages. Obtained input from department employees on which software would best meet their processing needs. Negotiated a discounted price on the software, installation and training costs. Coordinated transfer of data from paper records to new software. Supervised the installation of software over a weekend.

Results: *At the end of the year, department saved $80,000 and two people were assigned to different projects.*

Now trying writing your own.

Accomplishment No. 1

Short title:

Date and Place:

Challenge:

Actions:

Results:

Accomplishment No. 2

Short title:

Date and Place:

Challenge:

Actions:

Results:

Accomplishment No. 3

Short title:

Date and Place:

Challenge:

Actions:

Results:

USING YOUR TELEPHONE TO GET A JOB INTERVIEW

 Some Job Search Methods Work Better Than Others

It is important to use a variety of methods and most people do use more than one technique. What methods are best for you? Truth be told, every job search method works for some people. It is important to understand the different approaches and use what seems to work best for your situation.

The telephone can be one of the most efficient ways when you are searching for you next opportunity. You don't have to spend time on the road, and you can contact a large number of people in a short period of time.

Many job seekers say they get more interviews by using the phone than other networking methods. You can ask people you already know for names of employers, and then pick up the phone and call to request an interview. You can also just make the good old fashion cold calls from names you find in the yellow pages or on the Internet.

Making calls will require you to overcome being shy. Once you get use to making the calls, you will get use to it. It helps to develop a script to follow and write out the script the way you would actually talk:

Ask to be connected to the person in charge or if you have a name that was given by one of your contacts, ask for that person directly. If asked the what the reason of the call is, say it is business related...

"Hello, my name is _____(name of caller)." " I would like to speak to the person in charge of the _____(desired department)," please.

"Hello, Mr./Ms._____ If pertinent, give the name of person who suggested that you call..."Mr./Ms._____ Miller suggested I give you a call. I am interested in the current position you have open as _____(name of position).

"I am inquiring about the ad on (name job board, newspaper or, career service agency), regarding the_____(title of position). "If the person is in a hurry and wants to end the conversation..."I understand that you are very busy, but could we set up an interview at your earliest convenience? "If the person asks you to call back..."When is a good time for me to reach you? "

If the person wants more information... Give your elevator pitch and include work experience, training, skills..."I have worked____ (number of years) at___(agency name of former employer), where I___(past work activities related to skills in prospective job.)" or: "I have experience in_____(duties and work related activities). I am very interested in pursuing a career in____(field of related work)."Getting the interview... "I would like to set up an interview at your earliest convenience."

- Make sure to have your calendar at hand and some open dates.
- If you are rejected... "Might I come in and talk with you anyhow, or possibly drop off my resume, in case something opens up in the near future?"
- Do not ask for directions. Use MapQuest or Google the address and find directions.
- Ask for other leads... "Can you suggest any other places I could contact? Who would I speak to there?"
- Closing... "Thank you for your time."

Write your own...

_____
_____
_____
_____
_____
_____
_____
_____
_____
_____

PUTTING IT ALL TOGETHER - SUMMARY OF WHERE YOU ARE RIGHT NOW

JOB LOSS CYCLE

Circle the Nearest letter that best describes where you are right now in the job loss cycle:

Managing your transition. Circle the ones that need your most immediate attention right now and what you can do to improve that area.

1. Family
2. Friends
3. Job Search/Support Groups
4. Positive Thinking
5. Career Change/Retraining
6. Job Contacts
7. Survival Jobs
8. Do the Little Things
9. Exercise
10. Reduce Financial Pressure

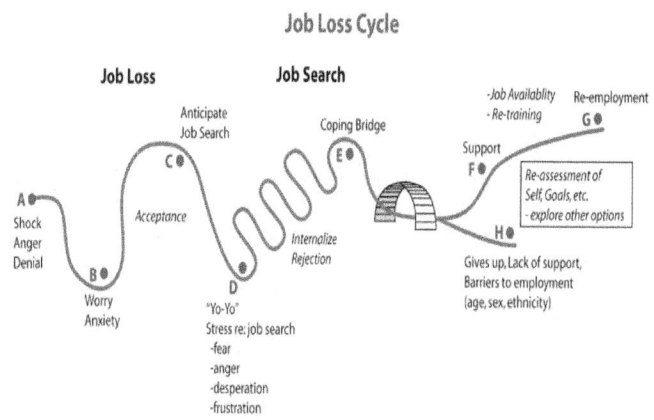

My plan for improvement in the area above: Be specific. (example: reach out to all my friends by the end of the week and let them know my situation and ask for help)

_____
_____
_____
_____
_____
_____
_____
_____
_____
_____

Top 5 Biggest Barriers	Ways to overcome barriers
1.	
2.	
3.	
4.	
5.	
Top 5 Concerns	**Ways to overcome concerns**
1.	
2.	
3.	
4.	
5.	
List the five most marketable skills	Are you most marketable skills ones that are a good fit for the type of position you are currently pursuing? If not, then what do you need for the type of position you are most interested in doing?
1.	
2.	
3.	
4.	
5.	
Top 5 personality traits	Are any of your personality traits detrimental to you success? If so, which ones and what can you do about overcoming them?
1.	
2.	
3.	
4.	
5.	
Top 5 Job Satisfaction Factors	Are the job satisfaction factors ones that you will most likely be able to use in the position you are looking for? If not, what positions would fit these factors?
1.	
2.	
3.	
4.	
5.	

Top 5 things you would like to include in your idea job

1.
2.
3.
4.
5.

Write out what your ideal work environment would be if you could incorporate all the things you want in your ideal job.

After narrowing my options, I have determined I want to be a:

_____ _____ _____ _____ _____ I am considering of Creating my own job and starting a business in?	What resources do I need?

SETTING GOALS TO REACH THE TARGET

By now you should have a definite target of the types of positions and companies, both for the short- and long-term, to map out your one page Job Search Campaign Master Plan. If you are not clear and don't have a focus, DON'T DO ANYTHING ELSE in your job search until you've thoroughly completed this step. You will be wasting your time if you are not clear on what you should be targeting or what you really want to do. If you are a person with a diverse background and have had many difference experiences, this can be challenging.

Make sure to do your homework and review some job openings and the descriptions of the jobs that are of interest you. You will begin to see specific job requirements repeated after you have looked at several job leads posted on job boards or company websites. These skills need to be the centerpiece to your resume, assuming you have those skills to begin with. If not, you are never going get past the first hurdle. Stop here and start over or find a way to get the skills! That might mean going back to school, maybe doing some volunteer work in that type of position or finding someone that will give you a chance to learn the skill on the job. The later is often the most challenging, since most employers can find people who can hit the ground running.

A good example is when a client I worked with wanted to be a physical therapist but was working in logistics at the time. We I asked him when he planned to start school for training to be a physical therapist, he said, "Oh, I don't have time for school." My response was, "well then; I guess you will not become a physical therapist. You cannot walk into a hospital and say, "gee, today I decided to be a physical therapist, but don't have any training.

Begin to Take Action

Consider what has to be done in relation to either your immediate or future job target(s)

Now ask yourself rather or not you have all the skills you need to do the job! If you don't have what it takes to do the ideal job you would like to have, you will have to determine the steps you need to take in order to be qualified for the type of job you want.

Determine the steps it will take to complete each action. I must take the following actions to be qualified for the position:

Action (take a class, get a certification, volunteer, find someone to give me the chance to learn on the job, etc.)	Target Date	Done

YOUR REASON FOR LEAVING YOUR LAST POSITION RESPONSE

One question you will begin to hear from friends, neighbors, and colleagues may already be asking you, "What happened with your job?" It is most necessary that you be prepared to handle this question — regardless of who asks it. So one of the first things you will want to develop is a response that is truthful and comfortable to you, and to your previous and prospective employers.

Most likely edit your "Reason for Leaving Response" several times. Although you will not distribute your written copy, this process will keep your explanation concise, to the point and help ensure that you have it planted firmly in your mind.

When drafting your response, please consider these points:

- Keep It Short and Factual.
- Typically, the more you try to explain, the more difficult your response can sound. You should be prepared to answer the follow-up questions, but only if they are asked.
- Be As Positive As Possible.
- Negative statements about your former boss or company will only hurt you in the long run.
- Put Your Best Foot Forward, But Be Truthful.

There are a number of factors that lead up to someone leaving a job. Pick the reason that is most positive and easiest to explain.

Say something like…that's the hardest decision you ever had to make. You are appreciative for the opportunity your last employer gave you, but right now this decision will be beneficial for you and your previous employer as you want to have the opportunity for career advancement, and you are realizing your other potentials.

- "My work has become unexciting, I am looking for a more challenging position where I can apply my skills and experience more efficiently."
- Unless you were laid off, or the company had relocated too far, just say "it's a strategic career move." It's better not to go into the specifics.
- "I was looking for something more challenging." Also, if you couldn't get along w/ your old boss, don't say negative things about him/her; say that, unfortunately, you and your old boss had some disagreements, and it was a mutual decision for you to move on.
- Tell them why you left! If it were particularly unpleasant, remember that they can always check references.

You could always say: It was time to move on due to (no advancement), more money, better benefits, location closer to home, seeking a job that is a better fit, seeking a job that more closely relates to your career goals.

A good example: "After working for 5 years in my previous profession or position, I recognized that I really wanted to work with X and my prior job didn't have any X." Where X is something that your interview company has. This is a good response because it shows that there was a valid cause for your leaving and that you think ahead, and that you are not just interviewing at their company because you want a job, but that the new company has something you want, and you will be a motivated worker.

Now write your Reason for Leaving Last Position Response:

_____
_____
_____
_____
_____
_____
_____
_____
_____
_____
_____
_____

NETWORK, NETWORK, NETWORK

Despite latest innovations, the fundamentals of building an effective network remain unchanged and networking can result in thousands of great contacts that can help you reach your destination.

- While networking may seem like a recent trend — aided by the explosion of technology-enabled platforms there is an art of building and maintaining personal and professional relationships, and it is as old as time.
- Offering Help Before Asking for It. To be an effective networker it is always better to give before you take.

This approach will give you a position of response and appreciation, and when you do ask for help, you will get your requests filled faster than if you have a tendency to always ask before you give.

CONTACT / NETWORK DEVELOPMENT OVERVIEW

The Main Important Goals in Networking

1. **Select good contacts**. You can always start your networking efforts with anyone you know who knows people and are willing to talk to you. But a better strategy is to start with people who know, like and trust you. Select family members and close friends who are likely to have good contacts or are familiar with the type of work you want. The contacts they refer you to will be likely to know even more about what the job you are targeting, or have even better contacts. As you gain more and more contact names from everyone you talk to, you network will grow quickly and before you know, you will find those who hire people with your skills or know of someone who does.

2. **Always present yourself professionally**. Convincing a warm lead that you have the skills to do the job will be easier if you are able to present your value clearly and concisely. Plus your warm contacts must like you in order to get any assistance from them or if they don't like what they hear and see it will be very difficult to get help from them. Be prepared to tell your contacts what you are looking for that includes the type of position, what skills you have, your experience, and any other credentials to support your ability to do the job.

3. **Always ask for two more referrals**. Often a warm contact will know of an opening for someone with your talents and interests but not always. Your goal is to get the names of at least two more people who could help you in your job search campaign.

I call this building your personal sales team. The more people, who know, like and trust you and have a clear idea of what you want, will start to network for you!

If you ask the right questions, you will get great referrals. There are three essential questions to ask each contact referral you talk to.

1. Do you know of anyone who might have an open position in my area of expertise? If the answer is no, then ask…

2. Do you know of anyone who might know of someone that would? If the answer is still no, then ask…

3. Do you know anyone is has a lot of connections?

All though most job seekers get contacts from friends and relatives, most job seekers do not use their contacts with people they know in an organized and systematic way. They get names of people without asking the right questions and often spend a lot of time talking to the wrong types of contacts. By asking the three questions above you will get much better results. They work!

Check If You Are A Member In This Group	Other Groups You Are Part of
Friends	
Relatives	
Friends of parents	
Past coworkers	
Members of my church	
People who sell me things (store clerks, insurance agent, realtor, etc.)	
Neighbors	
People I graduated with or went to school with	
Former teachers/ professors	
Members of professional associations or other social clubs	
People who provide me services (hair dresser, auto mechanic, etc.)	
Members of sports or other hobby groups	

Once you have completed this, you might be surprised by the number of potential warm contacts you already have. Even if you don't know some of them very well or at all, you still have something in common with them. It is a way to start a conversation with them. If you are shy, this may take some courage, but you can do it! You will find that most people want to help out if you ask them.

If you take the first person on your list for example and ask that person for the names of two people, you will have two new contacts. If you continue this process, your network will continue to grow beyond belief. If you can imagine, if you kept getting two referrals from each person, you would have 1, 024 in your network after the tenth level of contact. Just by starting with one person! Once you have created your list above, then you should create a list of each group on a separate list.

Networking Worksheet – Past Coworkers List

How many past coworkers do you have? Don't limit yourself to the most recent position; go back as far as you can remember. Write the number here _____ Now list as many names as you can below.

Name	Phone Number and / email / LinkedIn profile

Sample Cover Letter to Contacts

Hi Dave,

It's been a while since you and I have touched based. I just wanted to give you a quick update about things going on in my professional life.

Unfortunately I was informed, last week, by the company that I work for that, as part of an organizational restructuring, I'd be losing my job effective immediately. Although I'm shocked and disappointed by this, I'm going to hit the ground running looking for my next opportunity. This is a great wake-up call that nothing is permanent, and the security of long-term employment just isn't a reality for anyone these days.

I'm also taking this as an opportunity to re-evaluate my career, and how I can best to utilize my transferable skills or better yet consider looking into other possible industries or positions.

I have attached an updated version of my resume. Would you mind taking a look at it and give me some feedback? While you are reviewing it maybe you can think of some potential opportunities or businesses that I might want to focus my attention on based on my skills and experience. Your input would be greatly appreciated!

I'll keep you in touch and let you know how things are going. By the way, I've joined www.linkedin.com to expand my personal marketing exposure efforts, and noticed that you're also a member so let's definitely connect. Also, if I see any of your contacts that I might want to connect with, would you be open to making an introduction?

Again, if you have any other ideas for me to help my job search be more productive feel free to provide information and feedback. Here's my latest contact information and please me your latest information, and I'll update my records too.

Thanks,

John Doe

2345 Lakeshore Drive

Cleveland, OH

Home: (555) 123-5684

Cell: (555) 576-0796

Email: DoeJ578@gmail.com

LinkedIn Professional Profile: www.linkedin.com/ XXXXX

Web Portfolio: www.myexecutiveweb.com/johndoe

PREPARING A 30-SECOND ELEVATOR PITCH

Among the essential tricks to successful interviewing and networking is to create a really strong impression. One of the initial opportunities to make this impression is frequently in response to the "Tell me about yourself". The reply is your individual "commercial". It is essentially a very short summary and introduction of your skills, abilities, strengths and targets, all in about 30 seconds!

When will I utilize it? You will certainly use your 30-2nd pitch throughout your professional life. Some pertinent uses include:

- At a job interview.
- In a cover letter to highlight your capacities and expertise.
- When you are asked to introduce yourself at professional networking events.
- When calling companies for a future job opening.
- When presenting yourself to a prospective company at a job fair.

Exactly what should I feature in my 30-2nd pitch? The framework of a 30-2nd pitch typically follows this layout or design:

- Present yourself, when appropriate.
- Include your experience. State an expertise in which would be most memorable.
- Share an accomplishment or two that shows you have the ability. It could be associated with college or work, a volunteer encounter, a task like Coaching| or Training football, and so on.
- Explain your job search objective. Include just what you are searching for in a future position?
- Most importantly, state exactly how you could instantly, bring value to the business and hit the ground running.

Just what should I bear in mind regarding creating my 30- 2nd pitch?

Practice, practice, and practice your 30- 2nd pitch until you are comfortable and it sounds natural. Although prepared ahead of time, it should never ever seem memorized. You want to appear confident, positive, enthusiastic and comfortable at the same time while keeping your professional composure.

Make it unforgettable but yet not too far over the top. You are contending with lots of other qualified prospects. Your pitch needs to stand out and attract attention from the crowd. Whether it is the language you choose or a particular achievement you point out, you want to involve the audience and provide a chance to see your individuality.

Be ready for follow-up inquiries, particularly if this is a job interview. You could be asked additional details or to clarify something you stated or claimed which would certainly keep the discussion going. Part of your technique should be to create a connection with the interviewer, a recruiter or group of people at networking events and a great pitch will certainly assist in doing that and in establishing a memorable, lasting impression.

Vary your closing to match the circumstances. For a job interview concentrate on how you could benefit the company or exactly how you match the particular position is appropriate. At a networking event including Job Fairs, you want to be proactive and may consider asking questions such as, "Would it be ok with you to send you a resume?" or "Can I have your business card and call you...".

Questions to think about in creating your 30-2nd pitch:

1. What exactly what is your professional goal? (Typically it would involve doing something for a company).

2. Just what capability or experience do you have that would certainly support or capture that target?

3. What exactly are your accomplishments or experiences that show you have that skill and experience to be successful doing the job?

4. Exactly what are you looking} for in a job?

5. How can you directly help the company?

For Instance: Perhaps if you were applying for a position in sales you might say something like:

"I am a refined professional with documented evidence of excellence, a 4-year degree in marketing and advertising, and genuine ability to promote and market your products and the ability to close the deal with people at all levels, if offered the opportunity to do so. I am here today due to the fact that I recognize your need and have the credentials and necessary skills for the position and ability to make both of us benefit in the process."

Maybe you are going to interview for the position of supervisor. In this instance you could claim something like:

"As an efficient supervisor, I have the potential to select, lead, work with, fire, encourage, and coach groups individuals at any level. My teams have actually succeeded in being given various honors in the past because of my continuous support and management style. I would certainly like the opportunity to review my unique and distinct capacity to help you and make your sales team a cohesive team that will certainly function well with each other and cooperate to make your business expand continuously no matter what the economic climate might be.".

Now write your own…

I am a _____ with _____ years of experience

in _____ and _____.

My ability to

_____

Also I am

_____

Currently I am looking for an opportunity to

_____

_____

_____

Again my name is

_____ and

I can be reached at

_____

ONE PAGE JOB SEARCH CAMPAIGN MASTER PLAN

The success of your Job Search Campaign is dependent on how well you have prepared your self-promoting marketing materials and how consistently you execute your Job Search Campaign Master Plan. If you manage it like the full-time job it really is, you will eventually achieve success. If you handle it nonchalantly and pursue your plan on a hit-or-miss or part-time basis, you are likely to get discouraged and eventually settle for something less than you would usually expect.

Having a detailed, well-designed plan is helpful in keeping you focused and well organized. But the real benefit of having a plan is to channel hard work into identifying your primary target market and systematically working to put yourself in front of the key decision makers for a job interview in organizations you have chosen as one of your targets.

When you finally get to the Job Interview phase, you will know more about the business, its markets (and hopefully its management) and rivals than many people who work there. As you build Your Personal Job Search Campaign Master Plan, don't forget that there is a set of methods, like, in a sale's, that must be followed. People who just send their resume unexpected are sidestepping a number of very important steps and are making it virtually impossible to close the right sale. It's like playing the lottery. It is a hit and a miss!

SAMPLE ONE PAGE JOB SEARCH CAMPAIGN MASTER PLAN

PROFESSIONAL OBJECTIVE: Senior Corporate Finance Director/Treasurer

Contribute to the financial direction and success of a sizeable company. Lead and implement capital market and treasury undertakings as well as financial and business dealings. Provide extraordinary reporting to key stakeholders and senior management. Provide financial analysis and support of new business prospects, business process development and improvement. Evaluate and communicate company-wide financial information through assessment of ongoing financial performance with forecasts, budgets, and reports.

Positioning Statement: Recent graduate of top MBA with work experience at prominent Wall Street firms Goldman Sachs and Citigroup in investment banking and treasury transactions. Excelled at financial structuring and analysis and in delivering high value solutions to organizations. Demonstrated ability to work well independently and as a team member and interact with all levels of staff and management. Enjoy solving problems and identifying key issues and relationships from a diverse set of data.

COMPETENCIES/STRENGTHS

TARGET MARKET

Financial	Organizational Skills	Problem Solving	Attributes
Modeling company financials	Effective written and verbal communication skills	Project completion	Goal-directed nature
Cash management techniques	Supervising analytical projects and staff	Gathering and analyzing	Excellent interpersonal skills
Valuations	Presentation skills	Identification of key issues, objectives and relationships	Team player and Leader
Budgets, cash flow analysis	Project management	Development of solutions and plan for implementation	Energy & enthusiasm
Credit transactions	Coordination and completion		Self-motivated
Company/ Industry analysis			Customer-focused
Scenario/Sensitivity	Establishing and meeting deadlines		

Geographic: Washington D.C., Maryland, Virginia, North Carolina, South Carolina, Georgia—Metropolitan areas or academic centers

Types of Industries: Healthcare (including pharmaceutical), Retail/Consumer, Media/Telecom, Financial Services, Energy

Size of Organization: Fortune 1000 /Company has large finance department that involves broad areas of finance

Organizational Culture: Atmosphere where collaboration and information sharing and high standards are prized and rewarded. Culture respects a balanced lifestyle

TARGET LIST

Healthcare	Retail/Consumer	Media/Telecom	Financial Services	Energy	Regional
GlaxoSmithKline	Williams-Sonoma	Clear Channel	Capitol One	Duke Energy	UPS
Quintiles	Ukrop's	Media General	Jefferson	Southern Co.	Marriott
Trigon Healthcare	Circuit City	BellSouth	Bank of America	Dominion Resources	Delta
Coventry Healthcare	Home Depot	Washington Post	Fannie Mae	Progress Energy	CSX Corp.
Anthem	Lowe's	Discovery Communications	Freddie Mac	ExxonMobil	Norfolk Southern

Marketing Plan example from the Armstrong Center for Alumni Career Services at the University of Virginia Darden School Foundation.

MAXIMIZING YOUR EXPOSURE TO OPPORTUNITY AND DECISION MAKERS

Using Marketing Channels and Multiple Strategies Simultaneously

Keep in mind that you have additional sources to locate opportunity and market intelligence, including further online investigation, blogs, social media sites such as www.linkedIn.com, Facebook, Twitter, industry-specific discussion forums, trade associations, trade journals, and dialogue with influencers in venues such as informational meetings, and the research department of your local library.

Comparison of how a Human Resource Manager will look at a job candidate differently than a Key Decision Maker.

Human resource manager: HR persons use criteria filters such as industry experience, education, etc. They will look at how you fit a job description. A person with your background and skills cannot afford to be "short-circuited" by a lower level HR person.

Key decision maker: Decision makers look at profit. They will look at how you will contribute to increasing revenues, profits and better customer / client relationships. Their focus will be on how you can help them be a better organization, rather than how you will fit a job description.

USE OF SOCIAL MEDIA IN JOB SEARCH CAMPAIGNS

Finding Unadvertised Opportunity through Strategic Contact Development
Using the Power of Social Media

Social media in business is about gaining trust and building relationships. It is the same with job hunting. Recruiters post positions on various social networks such as LinkedIn.com, Twitter.com and Facebook because the platforms allow for multiple candidates to reach out to them with little-to-no advertising cost.

Recruiters and decision makers use social media to uncover top talent, locate those who are contributing content (thought leadership), and professionals who are proving to be relevant to the marketplace. They can instantly discover who are the industry's influencers, "follow" them to track what they are saying / working on, and then connect with them.

Social media usage constructs a "funnel" to capture recruiter / employer attention by creating a reason for dialogue through the exploration of mutual interests. There are three main factors to secure the sale in the sales funnel (your hiring): Lead Generation, Lead Cultivation, and Lead Conversion.

- Lead Generation: As a candidate in a job search, your greatest need to ensure your greatest success will be in creating a sound "Lead Generation" source. This lead generation is the portal to create awareness of you and your talents. Active participation in targeted social media venues such as LinkedIn and Twitter, or discretely and professionally using YouTube to display your knowledge, develops a "top-of-mind" awareness of your interests, competency and industry relevancy.
- Lead Cultivation: Once you have created a pipeline that ensures a steady supply of "leads," the next phase of your sales / marketing funnel is "Lead Cultivation." This is where you begin to build a relationship with recruiters, decision makers and influencers who have found you through your online presence through social media and offline dialogue. It is also where you position yourself as the best solution for their needs; you generate a need for your talents.
- Lead Conversion: Similar to the selling of a product, the subsequent components of your sales / marketing effort as a job hunter must focus on "Lead Conversion." Your consistent, proactive and relevant contribution on the top social media platforms which demonstrate your thought leadership and intuitive sense of your industry's emerging trends, will develop leads, forge dialogue with recruiters and employers, generate market demand for your talents, and convert interest into interviews.

The Wikipedia defines a sale's funnel as: "A sales funnel is constructed by stacking several layers together." Your job search from the bottom up will look just like this with the "sale" being the actual hire. How recruiters will use social media is shown in this diagram. Note the engagement, the two-way connectivity, between you and them (Seek, Secure, Solve, Sale):

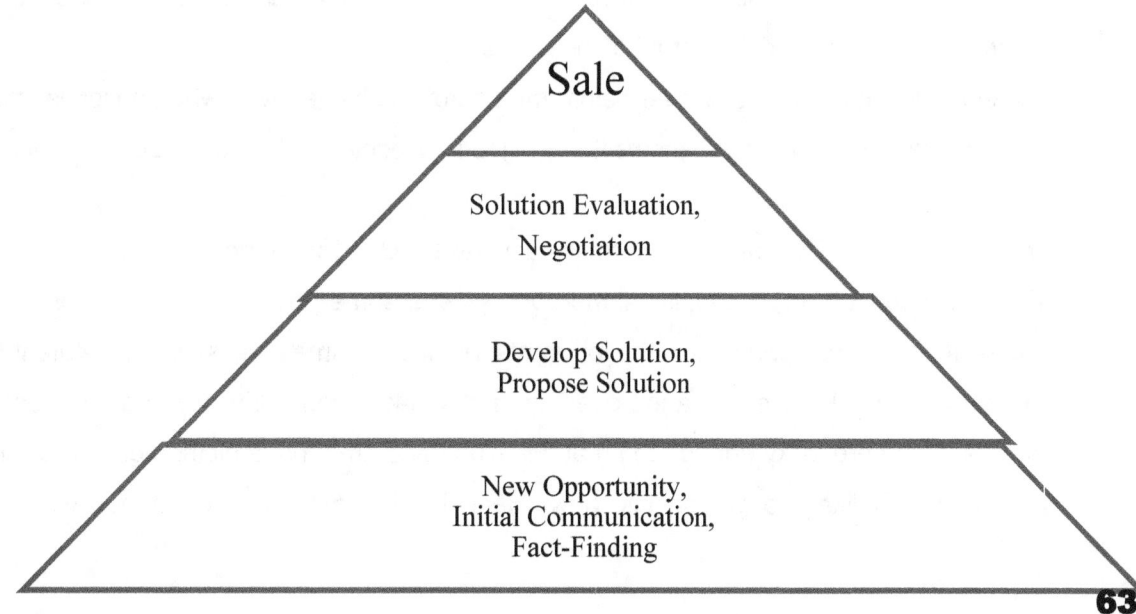

With the widespread recruiter migration from using job boards and other avenues to find top talent to sourcing on online social media platforms such as LinkedIn (primarily), Twitter and Facebook is driven by a need for increasing hiring efficiency. They have significantly improved their business productivity through use of social media because online profiles are more fluid, adaptable and scalable as compared to the static resume.

Anyone in the position of hiring that deploys social media as a recruiting tool has at his / her fingertips, a number of apps to conduct a search with more accuracy and gets better results. They also can conduct stealth- like precision pre-screening activities such as reference checking, reviewing what others say about a candidate, and what the potential candidate does in his / her off hours. The "package" a recruiter is able to pull together on a prospect is akin to creating a comprehensive dossier, and all this is done, prior to an actual first contact with a potential candidate, which in turn considerably streamlines the process.

THERE ARE 4 STAGES TO JOB OPENINGS

1. There is no opening: Often when you call a company and ask an employer if they are hiring, the answer is no. So, if you were using the traditional methods of job searching, you wouldn't even talk to the employer. Yet, if there is an opening in the future, the employer will consider people he or she already knows.
2. No formal opening exists, but people who work at the company knows a job may soon be available: When businesses start to pick up or there are plans to launch a new product, insiders know there will be openings in the near future. Maybe someone is getting ready to retire, or getting fired or moving out of state. Again, if you ask the boss in this stage if there are any openings you will most likely hear the word "no". So, most job seekers will continue to look and only advertised positions, not seeing the job that was about to open right in front of their eyes.
3. Someone who knows an employer before the end of this stage, even when no job is officially open, but someone inside the company knows that the job is expected to be open soon will once again fill these jobs.
4. An opening exists, but has not be formally advertised: Due to the growth of the business or the launch of a new product or other situations, the boss says at some point; there is a job opening. So, people who work for the company know the job exists, but it sometimes takes weeks before it is advertised. If you happen to ask if there is a job opening in this stage, you will finally hear yes, as a matter a fact there is. If you are lucky enough to be at this place and time, have all the right skills and experiences, you are highly likely to get an interview. Here lies the problem. For those who only search for

advertised openings, will never discover these types of opportunities. Someone who knows the business will fill them quickly.

Advertised position: If there isn't someone on the inside to fill the job, or by an insider referral or even someone the boss knows, it will ultimately be advertised to the public. An employer might post it on the Internet, run an ad in the local newspaper or even hang up a sign in the window. So for those who are looking for open positions, they likely hood of dozens or even hundreds of people could apply for it. That is why the competition for advertised positions is so competitive and fierce.

A savvy job seeker will get to employers at all levels of the stages of openings. This means you must contact employers in the first three phases before the public knows the position is open. Don't overlook advertised openings; of course; just be aware that most jobs will not be advertised. This is one method that has been proven to work better than more traditional methods of job search.

Three Benefits of Using a Spot Opportunity as a Chance to Talk Directly to Key Decision Makers

1. A letter goes out to the hiring manager or other key decision makers for the company. You are differentiating your method from your competition by implementing this unique advertising effort. The letter shows you really want to work for them. Using direct access strategy allows you to talk about the potential for the company by saying, "I see your company is doing launching a new product or the CEO is retiring or whatever the case maybe and with my background; we should talk."
2. Follow up with a phone call to the hiring manager or other decision makers. Obviously, since the company has established a need that they have (identified through research, and they know you are aware of the situation at hand), if you handle the call well enough , you can create a chance for a meeting.

    This meeting is usually 3-6 months ahead of the traditional, overcrowded external postings, Internet or recruiter" approaches. (These approaches are expensive for companies to utilize, consuming a lot of time reviewing hundreds of resumes from "outsiders" and extremely labor-intensive).
3. The Spot Opportunity method saves the company time and money and can be designed to the company's needs, requiring little to no work on the company's part.

Other thoughts to consider based on your circumstances are:
4. Stay focused on the company needs and explains with examples of your (accomplishments) how your skills and experience will help build value and a win-win for the company.
5. Value could include increasing profits, reducing costs, improving productivity, etc.
6. The employer will appreciate the research and strategizing completed before hand and before focusing on negatives. Take advantage of the positive impression you have made. Using this type of approach is one of the fastest ways to be aware of the unpublished openings.

The Spot Opportunity letter you will develop allows you to present yourself to the hiring manager and other decision maker as a person who can solve their problems. The following Spot Opportunity letter, when you customized to the requirement-hiring manager, will be a good working prototype.

Sample Letter – Spot Opportunity

John T. Doe

98765 South Waterside Drive, Any City, Any State 34587

Mobile: (555) 123-4567 • Email: Jdoe@comcast.net
Professional Profile at: www.linkedin.com/in/johndoe

Digital Portfolio: www. / johndoe@sbcglobal.net

Date

Herbert Jackson, Vice President of Operations
Mid-Atlantic Development Corporation

1234 Columbia Road

Washington, D.C. 20007

Dear Mr. Jackson:

I just read in the Washington Post that your firm has opened an office in Washington and will develop several properties that have been acquired. My experience in planning and managing construction projects may be useful to your company as it begins to develop these properties.

I have ten years of experience in the management of major commercial and industrial ventures. I am looking for an opportunity to apply my expertise to market development, pre-construction planning, and construction management with a development firm.

My track record of accomplishments has been in the management and design of multi-million dollar construction projects where I have successfully applied my management and technical skill in planning, bidding, negotiation, cost management, engineering, and construction. I have the technical knowledge, practical experience, and management capabilities necessary to develop new projects and markets, and provide an increased return on investment.

On a recent project, I managed the renovation of one of the largest high-rise apartment complexes in the Boston area. The plumbing and mechanical systems in the building were badly deteriorated, and asbestos had to be removed from many of the pipes. The work was successfully completed on schedule and within budget, while the tenants remained in their apartments. The owners benefited from maintaining the cash flow from rents, the job was profitable for my firm, and the success of this project and its wide exposure in the trade media have resulted in offers for new work for my company.

I will be following up shortly to see if my construction planning and management experience might be useful to Mid-Atlantic as it moves into the Washington area. Thank you for your consideration. You can view my professional profile at, www.linkedIn.com and by typing in my name in the 'Search People' function.

Sincerely,

John T. Doe

MARKETING CHANNEL EXPOSURE TECHNIQUE

Adjunct Market Exposure Channels: Contact Development & Spot Opportunities

www.linkedIn.com

LinkedIn is an online network of more than 4.8 million experienced professionals from around the world, representing 130 industries. LinkedIn Jobs is a relationship-powered job network that connects job applicants with the hiring managers, HR professionals or recruiters representing the jobs listed on LinkedIn. On LinkedIn Jobs, candidates not only find open positions that match their interests, but also get background information on the job poster that can help them tailor their cover letter. More importantly, job seekers can learn which of their existing professional contacts can introduce them to the hiring manager or recruiter — or to someone who knows these key contacts.

www.rileyguide.com

Go to the "A-Z Index" link and scroll through the headers to find relevant business and job search resources. This is the most comprehensive "one-stop-shop" of useful information, directories, and market intelligence. Due to its volume, best way to maximize its capabilities is to first make a master list of the header link titles that interest you. Then, return to each of them to see what it houses inside.

www.crain.com

Crain Communications is primarily a publishing company providing vital business news and information to industry leaders and consumers with 30 titles. Each newspaper, magazine and news Web site has become required reading and an authoritative source in its own sector of business, trade and consumer market.

http://biz.yahoo.com/industry/

Yahoo Industry News is excellent for competitor research. All the news about leaders and laggards within the industry is here. Solid portal for leads via spot opportunities.

http://www.business.com/directory/index.asp

Developed by a team of industry experts and library scientists, the Business.com directory contains more than 400,000 listings within 65,000 industry, product and service subcategories. So whether you're seeking general industry background or specifics about a particular product line, Business.com will deliver the most useful and relevant results every time.

www.bizjournals.com

The national Bizjournals' site features local business news from around the nation, updated throughout the day, top business stories from American City's print editions, and industry-specific news from more than 40 industries. Characterized among the "Best of the Web" by Forbes magazine, Bizjournals' archives contain more than 750,000 business news articles published since 1996. E-mail offerings include daily local business updates from any Bizjournals market, as well as weekly updates of industry news from throughout the country.

http://groups.google.com/

Google Groups is a free online community and discussion group service that offers the Web's most comprehensive archive of Usenet postings (more than a billion messages). They have recently added a number of features that make Google Groups an even more effective way to communicate with groups of people online.

www.google.com

Running Google "News" queries for the industry and position identifies spot opportunities for local and out-of-state cities.

http://blogsearch.google.com/   or....
http://search.blogger.com/

Blog Search is Google search technology focused on blogs. Your results include all blogs, not just those published through Blogger; the blog index is continually updated, so you'll always get the most accurate and up-to-date results.

Contact Development

Building a network of personal and professional contacts is a highly effective way to uncover leads or clues to unpublished opportunities. In all probability, the person who offers you your next position will not be somebody whom you know personally, but, you may very well meet this person through somebody familiar to you.

Remember, you are *not* approaching people with the question "Do you know anyone who is hiring?" Rather, you are asking for advice and direction, as it is appropriate to your campaign.

- **YOUR ISSUE:** You need information about companies inside and outside your home base (where you live), which might need someone with your skills.
- **YOUR COMFORT STATEMENT:** Contact a national trade association, using the phone number on the website. Ask for a referral to a member in your target state. Contact that person and brainstorm with them about companies in the area, and which ones might suit you. Ask who else they would recommend you talk to.
- **YOUR COMFORT STATEMENT:** Go to association meetings (or network within virtual ones such as on Linkelin.com and others), with a list of the organizations you want to know more about and ask people if they are familiar with them. Also, ask where, besides the website, they believe you can get additional information. Ask them if there are other organizations they can suggest you consider or people you should contact. Mine market intelligence from LinkedIn.com, Twitter, Facebook, etc.

When pursuing local companies, which are easily commutable, the most effective way to approach contacts is to phone them to arrange a face-to-face meeting. You may also initiate the contact with a letter, and follow up with a phone call to ask for a personal meeting. Out-of-area meetups are best done through social media sites such as linkedin.com, or via industry-specific discussion forums and blogs where you can first contribute meaningful counsel / comment to others and then privately contact them for further pursuit. Note: On LinkedIn.com you can directly email KDMs (Key Decision Makers), particularly if you have joined a Group that they and you are in to network. Your message must be tight, precise and relevant.

ANSWERING PUBLISHED OPPORTUNITY: Responding to advertised positions will also be a part of your "multiple strategies" campaign. Advertised positions will present the greatest competition to you, the job seeker. Maximize your chances of landing in the "to-be-interviewed" pile by diligently following the marketing recommendations I have given you.

Use your cover letter to respond directly to the qualifications required in the advertisement. If the decision maker is surfaced, then treat the situation as a Spot Opportunity. Send a letter to this target and address the "need" that you have surfaced.

You should investigate open positions on the Internet as another marketing channel. Setting up online "alerts" to have fresh open positions delivered daily to your email as they are available will allow you to be job searching "24/7." Follow up is the key – make follow up calls within a week (3 – 5 days preferred).

There are three significant navigating devices that greatly affect the outcome of your job search marketing campaign:

1. Your written documents.
2. The way you present yourself in interviews — face-to-face, video and on the telephone.
3. Your expertise in using linkedin.com to create an online presence for recruiters, decision makers and other influencers to find you, and for you to make contact with them through a linkedin.com direct email.

Your resume covers significant accomplishments and also provides insights to your potential value to an employer. Each resume should be fine-tuned to the employer, position / opportunity, and method of communication. Your resume related cover letters and other written, or oral presentations should reinforce one another, presenting your knowledge, skills, abilities, and experiences in a way most appealing to a prospective employer.

Remember to provide a copy of your resume to all of your references and to selected members of your network. This keeps you fresh in their minds

Carry copies of your resume with you to interviews, trade shows, and while traveling so that you can take advantage of spot opportunities.

- Your resume is the key to your written documentation. It is designed it to highlight the qualifications and achievements that are most relevant to your job target.

NOW THE FUN PART…WRITING A RESUME THAT GETS INTERVIEWS

Once you have a clear focus on what you want to target, you can start writing your resume. In the past 10-15 years, technology has changed the way companies search for and attract job seekers, screen for potential candidates, and manage the entire hiring process. In today's technology driven job market, hiring managers use the Internet to attract job seekers that are a good fit; use automated online questionnaires to screen potential candidates and software that is called applicant tracking systems (ATS) to manage the hiring process.

As companies have taken huge steps to embrace the world of technology there are still a large number of job seekers who still use old style resumes that precede the Internet! Since the job market has changed so must you and your resume.

Resumes are a dime a dozen, so making yours stand out can be the difference of getting an interview or not. Creating an outstanding resume that stands out and makes someone say, "wow" and want to call you is no easy task. To achieve this, you must be able to answer 4 questions on your resume.

Ultimately, your resume has one goal: to get someone who wants to interview you. That could include a recruiter, hiring manager or HR generalist. It all depends upon the job you applied for and the structure of the organization. So, how do you get your phone to ring?

THE 4 QUESTIONS YOUR RESUME MUST ANSWER

Using a standard, chronological resume doesn't work in today's job market. You need a high-quality, value-based resume in order for you to stand out in the mob of resumes.

You have a limited amount of time to make a first impression – usually 10 - 15 seconds or fewer. Your resume is typically the first impression to a prospective employer and the only thing they have to inspect the possibility of first interviewing you and then hiring you.

Prior to the interview, hopefully you've taken the time before this to research the company, recognize what the company is looking for, and know how your resume fits that particular situation. Make sure that your resume is written – not for you – but the reader in mind, and this would be the employer. In other words, think like the hiring manager and ask yourself, "would I hire me?" Are you meeting his needs or just listing your previous job description?

There are four critical questions that a quality; value-based resume needs to address. These answers will be seen from the employer's perspective – he wants to know the value you will bring to his company:

From the perspective of the recruiter or hiring manager, your resume needs to answer:

1. Who are you and what will you do to benefit our business?
2. How are you better qualified than other candidates?
3. What skills do you bring to the table that will allow us to believe the results you claim?

4. Where did you achieve the results in the past and can your produce future success in similar situations?

Think about it. What set you apart from all other job seekers? Why are you better than the 100 other people who've applied for the same job opportunity? That's the information you need to include on your resume. That's your unique selling point that gets the phone to ring.

Don't just think about and include the day-to-day, boring tasks that you do to pass the time between 9:00 am and 5:00 pm. Think about the great things you've delivered over the progression of your career. Your Victories + Awards + Tributes + Trainings = Your Greatness.

Recruiters and hiring managers see a whole lot of ordinariness in resumes that people send in and don't take the time to highlight what they can do for the company. It is liking reading an obituary! Take yours from being a chronologic obituary of what you have done to dazzling by focusing on what truly makes you better than any other potential candidate.

HOW DO YOU STAND OUT IN THE MOB OF RESUMES?

Every resume needs a clear focus that instantly tells a hiring manager what job or type of job the candidate seeks and what his or her top selling points are. In other words, you resume must be value based and straight to the point.

For many years, the objective statement functioned as the purpose of providing a starting point for resumes. Objectives nonetheless are out of style with employers because they inadequately written, indistinct, and is all about the job seeker. Job seekers also often viewed the objective as an invitation to list everything wanted, desired, and needed from the job, instead of a chance to describe potential contributions to the employer's bottom line.

Before we address the Resume Focus as the substitute for the objective statement, it's crucial to understand that employers today expect resumes to be tailor-made to the targeted position. In other words, you do not send the same resume in response to each job you target; you tweak it to align with each job. You do not need to rewrite all of -- or even most of -- your resume for every job you apply for, but you do need to adjust it to show that you are a fit for any position you are seeking.

Looking at Above the Fold

Above the fold" refers to the location of an important news story on the top half of the front page of a newspaper or on the part of a web page that is visible on screen without scrolling. Let's think about it, we pick up the newspaper, or open up a news focused web page, and the 1st thing we do is scan the top headlines to determine what stories are of interest to us.

Apply the "Above the fold" concept to the develop your resume, using headlines so that potential employers can immediately discover your experience, expertise and accomplishments at the top of your first page and be compelled to read more about you.

Resume headlines

Your headlines should be bold, clear and concise. Prove your value by painting a panoramic picture of your career - directed solely toward the job you are seeking.

Keep your "Above the fold" fresh

Resumes are dynamic marketing tools that should be reviewed and edited for each job that is targeted – and this takes dedication and hard work.

Think about Dunkin Donuts for a minute. Why do we all know the Dunkin Donuts (DD) brand so well? DD is not stagnant in its approach to building and maintaining a large customer base. Their marketing campaigns promote varied and ever changing beverages and menu items targeting different groups of people with diverse tastes, desire, needs and lifestyles. DD motivates many of us to be loyal customers.

Each time you prepare your resume in application for a job, think of yourself as a DD marketing executive. How can you appeal to a potential new customer (employer)? How can you convince an employer that you will meet or exceed specific needs and be the best choice as a new employee?

Transform your resume

Use Headlines to Attract Interest | Prove Your Related Value | Motivate Employers to Hire You

You can replace that with a headline that describes your value, such as:

- Sales Pro — Know for Exceeding Quota Month after Month for a sales professional who has consistently surpassed sales goals, -or-
- Certified Project Management Professional — for a project manager who wants to play up a critical certification.

How do you do that? Start With a Resume Headline and Professional Summary That Gets Their Attention and Passes the 10-second Look.

Another example of what "above the fold" might look like in a resume:

JOHN BROWN

address and/or phone number, email address,

and the URL for a social networking profile

Quota-Smashing Sales Pro

Highly qualified sales professional with strong, unfailing track record of success in the engineering industry. Surpassed quarterly sales quotas 90 percent of the time, earning four written acclamations from two CEOs. Helped increase revenue 10 percent a year over the past 5 years by assertively pursuing new customers from top contenders. Proven talent to support customers' individual needs to help ensure repeat business and higher share of wallet.

If I'm a sale's manager in an engineering firm and I need someone to help increase revenue and pick up new customers, I'd at least be captivated in reading more about this candidate, specifically the accomplishments that support this statement.

To enhance you're your chance of being invited in for an interview, pique the hiring manager's interest by taking the "above the fold" approach: Highlight what you can do and how you've done it, which can give the hiring manager plenty of reasons to read the rest of the resume and a clear picture of what your can offer an employer.

Effective resumes show a clear picture of the value you'll bring to an employer right off the bat. The Headline and Summary sections of your resume are a good place to start creating this picture. Resume users who have a Headline are more than twice as likely to be contacted by an employer as those who don't have one.

Think of the Headline as a professional tagline that includes:

- The type of job you're targeting and a description of your experience level
- Specific experiences or qualities that relevant and that the employers will value

Here's an example of an effective Headline and Summary section:

Headline: PRODUCT / BRAND MANAGEMENT AND MARKETING

Strategic positioning and management of a multi-line, international brand name with an emphasis on new product development, marketing and sales.

Summary:
- Gifted product/brand management professional with wide-ranging consumer product experience in the U.S., Latin America and Japan.
- Strong record of developing and executing state-of-the-art brand positioning strategies across numerous product categories that result in long-term brand equity maximization.
- Proven knack to manage product development/production procedures from concept through finished product, with close attention to budgets, time frames, quality and product stipulations.
- Well-honed presentation and negotiation skills within a multi-national environment.
- Fluent in French with basic conversational ability in Japanese.

If you have concentrated training or certifications that are commonly described with abbreviations, don't assume that recruiters will know their meaning. Put abbreviations in parentheses after the spelling out the words to ensure these qualifications aren't overlooked.

It should go without saying, but resumes with spelling mistakes or grammatical errors are likely to cause recruiters and hiring managers to stop reading. After carefully proofreading your resume, have a friend or colleague review it to help catch errors you may have missed.

Use Branding Statements

These statements delineate who you are, your worth, and why you should be called into an interview. A branding statement is a hard-hitting statement that tells the reader instantly what you can bring to an employer. Your branding statement should capture your reputation, showcase what sets you apart from others, and describe the added value you bring to the table. Think of it as a sales pitch. Consider incorporating these elements into the brief summation that is your branding statement:

- What makes you different?
- What qualities or characteristics make you unique?
- What have you accomplished that sets you apart from others?
- What is your most noteworthy personal character trait?

Don't be afraid to use the employer's name in your branding statement, for example: "Enthusiastic to lead ground-breaking strategic marketing initiatives that assertively increase Goodyear's market share, sustain growth, and maximize profitability."

Resume Headline in Combination with Branding Statement

Here's one example:

DIRECTOR, OPERATIONS

Focus in raising the bar, creating tactical approaches, managing high-risk situations, and cultivating the quality and performance of operations.

Turn Resume Objectives into Branding Statements

You may already have a well-written objective statement; it's not hard to adapt it to a Resume Focus that employers will pay attention to. Just eliminate the word "Objective." Then amend the language; take out the infinitive phrase -- "To play key role ...", "To provide ...", "To lead ...", "To increase ...", "To add value ..." -- that objective often start with.

Here are two examples of objectives converted to "objectiveless" objectives:

Objective: To produce an out-of-the-box foresight to an accelerated position on a ingenious marketing team with particular interest in copywriting.

Revised Resume Focus: Producing an out-of-the-box foresight to an accelerated position on a creative marketing team with particular interest in copywriting.

Objective: To improve company profits by contributing multilingual skills and expertise of civil-law countries in the legal department of a firm that engages in business in Latin America.

Revised Resume Focus Point: Dedicated to increasing company profits by contributing multilingual skills and knowledge of civil-law countries in the legal department of a firm that engages in business in Latin America.

Using a "Summary of Qualifications" or "Professional Profile" Section

Using this style, in a reader-friendly bulleted format lets your best selling points catch the potential employer's attention, and immediately establishes your value as a candidate.

If you use a section such as a Summary of Qualifications or Professional Profile, ensure that:

- it short and concise -- a maximum of 3-4 bullet points.
- It is not unsupported fluff. You must substantiate any skills or qualifications you excel at in this section by giving examples or evidence of how you demonstrated the qualification.

Resume Keyword Section

Keywords are extremely important for today's resumes because of Applicant Tracking Systems (ATS) and what they look for when resumes are placed in keyword-searchable databases after you submit them electronically. Keywords should be industry-specific and job-specific and taken right from the job posting.

A segment of keywords can use one of many potential headings, such as "Key Skills," "Core Competencies," "Key Proficiencies," and "Areas of Expertise." A big note of caution here: Keyword segments are useful on resumes when they are entered into Applicant Tracking Systems, but "disembodied" keywords do not rank as favorably in the systems as keywords used in context. "More advanced ATS systems will evaluate the framework in which each keyword is used and will give greater ranking to a keyword that is incorporated within the description of a career achievement, compared to one that is included in a keyword chart or some type of list." Thus, also consider keywords in bullet points in your Summary of Qualifications/Professional Profile, if you have one, and in the bullet points under each of your jobs.

Rest of Your Resume Must Be In-Line With Your Focus

While the top third of your resume's first page is the most important place for its Resume Focus, you can perfect the focus and the balance of your resume in various ways. You can decisively organize your resume to position you for the job you pursue. Remember that a resume is a promotional document that should highlight the qualities of your experience that best sells you for a specific position. You may also consider placing other sections of your resume before your experience section to stage your best selling features.

For example, do you have a MBA degree that adds value to your application? Or perhaps you speak 5 languages. All though speaking 5 languages is not part of the requirements; it certainly is a value ad and should be front and center.

You may want to re-prioritize the bullet points you present under each job, giving greater weight to an accomplishment that will be meaningful to the employer you're targeting. You've undeniably held jobs that embraced a broad scope, much responsibility, and many achievements. Tweak these to a razor-sharp list that are most relevant to the job you pursue next. Remove any bullet point that fails to support what you want to do next.

Best Ways of Adding Focus to Your Resume

The best way to make sure a Resume has a Focus and is clear throughout your resume is to ask yourself at every point in your resume preparation: What does the employer want to see? What information can I quickly convey that will show the employer how well I fit this job (or this type of job, or this industry)? What content should jump out at an employer spending just 10-15 seconds looking at my resume? Choosing that type of resume for your situation and your resume format is one of the first things you'll do when writing your resume. **The three most common types are:**

Chronological: Presents information in reverse order, most recent experience listed first and offers succinct picture of you as a potential candidate.

Functional: Focuses on specific assets and skills important to hiring managers.

Combination: All the flexibility and power of the functional and chronological combined.

All through have their pros and cons so make sure you choose the right format for your specific situation.

Others to consider

Mini Resume	Job searchers benefit from use of a Mini Resume because of its brevity, utility and portability. A synopsis of career achievements, industry-specific knowledge, credentials, and other qualifications is useful on a HyperCard (business card CD), recruiter inquiry email, references use request, online summary requirement, two-fold business card, or social and professional networking venues.
General Letter Resume	Job searchers who desire a quick interpretation of the relevancy of the skills to employer need, by decision makers, benefit from creating a tailored Letter Resume response because it highlights pertinent information about the company's business event or challenge, and his/her experience or capabilities. It is unnecessary to furnish complete details concerning a candidate's background. Liabilities can be suppressed and interview activity is increased as compared to standard resume approaches.
Proposal Letter-Resume	Job searchers will differentiate themselves if they approach decision makers,

	recruiters and persons-of-influence using a Proposal Letter-Resume that details a very specific solution to an identified business challenge. Proposal Letter focuses on the benefit of job candidate's competency and skills to increase revenues, streamline, upgrade, and move organization to next level of growth. Another use of a Proposal Letter is at job offer stage where a candidate creates a Counter Proposal Letter which provides an alternative and upgrade to the original job offer made to him / her.
Federal resume including KSAs, SES ECQs	Job searchers seeking Federal employment should use a resume specifically tailored for applying to Federal jobs as an option / replacement for standard submission of the streamlined Federal application, OF-612. A Federal resume sells a candidate's true value and benefit n greater depth than what is allowed on the brief OF-612 application. KSAs (Knowledge, Skill, and Ability) are written as standalone documents or to accompany a Federal Resume. Federal resumes and KSAs are custom-tailored documents targeted to a defined Federal job announcement / opening.
Electronic / Scannable Resume	Job searchers posting their resume online or responding to an employer request to transmit resume in Text form, will need to use an Electronic Resume because of its adaptability to electronic scanning systems and / or avoidance of sending resume as an attachment.

Final thoughts about writing an effective resume:

- **Write it yourself**. You can find samples in books and Google.
- **Make every word count and have meaning**. Limit your resume to one or two page. After writing a draft, edit it several more times. If a word or phrase does not support your ability to do the job, cut it out. Shorter is often better.
- **Make sure your resume is typo free**. One mistake on a resume can cost you the invitation to an interview and create a negative impression. Remember spell check does not catch everything. Read, then read it again and then have several other people read it and read it again!
- **Make it look fabulous**. Appearance and content are equal. If it appears sloppy or over the top, the first impression will be a lasting one and you will not get invited to an interview.
- **Stress Your Accomplishments**. A resume is no place to be shy or humble. Give facts, numbers and whatever else you can use to support your accomplishments in the best way possible.
- **Don't procrastinate**. Don't delay your job search campaign while creating and recreating a b "better" resume! Spending too much time trying to improve your resume can cost you an opportunity of landing the job you are looking for. The best approach is to do a simple, error-free resume and start the search. You can continue to improve your resume and still actively search.

Other things to consider:

Add a keyword section. A simple technique is to add a section to your resume titled "Key Skills" or Key Competencies." You can then add key words that may not be any place else in your resume.

Even an excellent resume won't get you interviews unless you use if effectively. In a keyword section you can add key words not included elsewhere in the resume.

Review job descriptions. Cautiously review job descriptions for the types of positions you are seeking. Key words can be found on corporate websites, reading industry trade magazines or checking out keyword resource books and websites and another great place is the O*NET Dictionary of Occupational Titles.

Be specific. List certifications and licenses only if they are relevant to the position you are seeking and include special language used in your field.

Keyword Examples

Keywords tend to be nouns that are specific industry qualifications, skills and abilities. Some keyword could include certifications, position titles, computer terms, industry jargon, product names, company names and professional organizations. You can always find key word examples by searching on the internet in your industry of choice.

And, lastly, if you're posting your résumé to a personal web page or résumé bank, be sure to hide your contact information from accidental viewers. Posting personal contact information on the web could attract unwelcome attention. To avoid this, activate the privacy settings offered on most résumé banks or by only providing an email address and just listing the city where you live on your web page and advocating employers contact you for additional information.

CREATING COVER LETTERS TO GET INTERVIEWS

Every time you send out a résumé you need to include a cover letter. Your cover letter will must be customized for each job you're applying for. This is just another way of introducing yourself to potential hiring manager. What it says about you can be the difference getting in front of people for an interview or not.

Choose the Right Format

Because people are busy they don't want to read long letters from people. It should be one page long, and in a standard business letter format. Make sure you match the font in the cover letter with the font in your resume.

Compose the Letter

First Paragraph: This is the most important part of the letter, so make it count. It will be the first thing your potential employer reads, so you will want to make a first great impression. Tell the reader how you heard about the job. This is especially necessary if you've been referred by a mutual acquaintance. Show excitement for the possible employment; then follow this with a few key qualifications you have that are pertinent to the position you're looking to obtain.

Second Paragraph: Describe your qualifications for the job – skills, talents, accomplishments and personal qualities. But don't go overboard. Only choose three of your top talents would make you stand out as a candidate. Don't repeat what's in the resume. When writing the cover letter, think about how you can contribute to the company and why your particular qualifications, talents, and achievements would be best for the position.

Third Paragraph: Describe why you think you'd fit the company – why it would be a suitable match. Maybe you like their products, or perhaps know people work there, or you've had the opportunity to visit their location or read about them in the paper. If the candidate feels some connection to the company and has a good understanding of how the company operates is a big plus and make the company feel more connected to you.

Fourth Paragraph: Mention the attached résumé, give them a reason to want to read it. (e.g., For my complete employment history and additional skills, please see the attached résumé) and make sure you ask for an interview. Suggest a time you plan to follow up. Make sure you give the ways to easily contact you such email, phone number and even include your LinkedIn profile link.

Suggestions for Creating Awesome Cover Letters:

- **Send it to someone by name if at all possible**: Call the company to see who the manager of the department you would be working in and make sure you get the persons correctly spelling and exact title. Sometimes you can find this information on the company website or through LinkedIn.

- **Be specific about what you want**. If you want an interview, ask for it. If you are interested in the company, say so. Give very clear and specific reasons why the company should consider you.

- **Be friendly and professional**. Avoid using the "hard-sell" hire me now approach. Using a professional yet more of an informal style is usually a better approach because people don't like to be pushed around.

- **Proofread carefully and make it look good.** Make sure you use good qualify paper and matching envelops. Consider sending your resume in a large envelop, addressed the person who is in charge, if you can get the name, had writer the address and return address and do not put "resume enclosed" on the envelop. Make it look like a personal piece of mail so it is more likely to end of up the desk of who it is intended for and not on the desk of the secretary who may not forward to the hiring manager and sent it to HR or trash it.

- **Target your letter**. Typical reasons for sending cover letters include responding to an ad, preparing an employer for an interview (best reason), and following up after a phone interview. Each letter has a different targeted reason so make sure you are clear and concise. Short and to the point is always best.

- **Follow-up**. Always remember when contacting an employer directly is much more effective than sending a letter. Don't expect your letters to get tons of interviews but if you contact an employer before hand that is when a cover letter is more effective. If you say you plan to follow up at a certain time, make sure you do that. That hiring manager just might be waiting for you call on that very date and time you stated in the letter!

DO-IT-YOURSELF-ER

If you consider yourself a "do-it-yourself-er" there are a lot of great books on the market that can help you craft a compelling and a visually distinct document. Here are a few of my favorites, including a couple on cover letters.

1. **101 Best Resumes to Sell Yourself – Introducing the Organizational Message Chart**, Jay Block (Author) This book is the most comprehensive book on HOW to market your value NOT your biography. This groundbreaking book explains how to transform a resume from a dry listing of employment history, education, and hobbies (a chronological obituary) into a dynamic, strategic, value-based tool. Outlining a step-by-step process for "personal branding" and separating yourself from your competition, this book introduces you to the Organizational Message Chart™ – the most powerful communications model (tool) ever devised for selling yourself. This resource offers dozens of tips, tactics, and techniques for professionally packaging and positioning you to attract the job you want at the pay you deserve.

2. **101 Best Cover Letters,** Jay Block (Author)
This book shows you how to create an image of accomplishment, professionalism, and competence that today's employers are begging for in the creation of a cover letter that properly introduces the resume! Job seekers have paid hundreds, if not thousands, of dollars for the expertise in this dynamic resource and regarded every cent as well spent! With these sample cover letters for any situation, you will be guaranteed that your resume will be read with interest and enthusiasm. Cover letters must NOT repeat what the resume communicates – it must build rapport with the reader. This extraordinary book shows you how.

3. **Resume Magic,** Susan Britton Whitcomb (Author)
Filled with "before and after" resume examples that not only teach the author's special method, but also show why they work. "Resume Magic" divulges the secrets of better resume writing from an expert with more than a decade of experience producing powerful, effective resumes.

4. **Expert Resumes for Career Changers,** Wendy Enelow and Louise M. Kursmark (Authors)
This collection of resumes is aimed at people who are transitioning from one career to another. The down economy has forced millions of people to change jobs or industries in order to stay

employed. This book gives strategies as well as 180 pages of sample resumes for successful career changes. The authors present sound resume-writing advice, including how to create and use an electronic resume. The appendix includes Internet resources for an effective online job search. New for this edition are completely updated resumes, a new chapter on writing cover letters, and a collection of cover letter samples.

5. **Best Resumes for $100K+ Jobs,** Wendy Enelow (Author)

   Individuals expecting to make more than $100,000 a year need to craft a very special resume that commands no only attention but a high salary as well.

6. **Expert Resumes for People Returning to Work,** Wendy Enelow and Louise M. Kursmark (Authors)

   A collection of professionally written resumes aimed at anyone who has left work for a period of time and then wanted to return. This type of situation requires a particularly unique approach to crafting a resume and presents some unique challenges.

7. In addition to nearly 200 pages of sample resumes, the authors present sound resume writing advice, including how to create and use an electronic resume.

8. **College Grad Resumes to Land $75,000+ Jobs,** Wendy Enelow, and (Author)

   This unique resume book includes 80 examples of resumes written by college students who actually obtained $75,000+ jobs in a variety of occupational fields. The book also includes sound resume writing advice based on the secrets of professional resume writers.

9. **Best Resumes & Letters for Ex-Offenders,** Wendy Enelow and Ronald Krannich (Author)

   Addresses special employment issues facing ex-offenders and provides sound advice on how to write, produce, distribute and follow up resumes and letters for overcoming employment barriers.

10. **Expert Resumes for Managers & Executives,** Wendy Enelow and Louise M. Kursmark (Authors)

    More than 100 professionally written resumes for people at all levels of management, from front-line supervisors to top-level executives.

11. **Best Resumes for People without a Four-Year Degree,** Wendy Enelow (Author)

    Addressing the unique resume needs of people without a bachelor's degree, this book meticulously illuminates what a resume is and is not, as well as what it should say, and how it should be presented.

12. **30-Minute Resume Makeover,** Louise Kursmark (Author)

    This book is for people who already have a resume and need to update it quickly for a new opportunity.

TIPS FOR SUCCESSFULLY INTERVIEWS

Have You Tried These Interview Tips?

- ☑ Dress professionally
- ☑ Have a firm handshake
- ☑ Make eye contact
- ☑ Research the company

Any of these pointers sound familiar? They should, because you've heard them thousands of times. While the above suggestions are great (and valid), the truth is that this kind of advice can get a bit common.

HERE IS THE STRATEGY THAT IS WINNING INTERVIEWS AND LANDING JOBS IN A COMPETITIVE JOB MARKET

By Eric Kramer– Founder Innovative Career Services and Author Active Interviewing™

"Active Interviewing is a great book. In today's climate, job seekers need as much help as they can get. Things have changed and it is not enough to simply send out a resume anymore. This book definitely gives you an advantage when it comes to finding a new job. It is written in a straightforward, easy-to-understand format, which I really like. While it is a large book (8 1/2 x 11, and almost 300 pages) it is a quicker read than it first appears. The author has broken the information down into many smaller sections, which makes it easy to digest the truckload of information, which this book contains. To me, this makes it easier to use and to comprehend the points that Mr. Kramer is trying to get across to potential job seekers.

This book is packed full of great tips about branding yourself, selling yourself to potential employers, and how to successfully present yourself during the interview process. Active Interviewing contain much too much information for me to try to list everything it covers in this review, so I will simply say that it is totally complete. I can't think of anything that this book leaves out. If you are looking for a job or just thinking of changing positions, I believe that you will find that this book has much to offer you and is well worth the price. I highly recommend this book to anyone who is going through the process of finding a new job. In my opinion, this book could just give you the edge that you need to be in control of your own destiny in the job market. Highly recommended!" Dr. Bohdi Sanders.

To learn more or buy a copy of the book visit: http://www.activeinterviewing.com

BEFORE THE INTERVIEW

All interviews have some similarities but not two interviews are exactly a like. Interviewers can make judgments about you even before you meet in person. For example, if you have had the opportunity to speak to the interviewer of even the receptionist by phone, or perhaps sent your resume or other correspondence. Be very cautious about early contacts with the employer. Always do your very best to make a great first impression.

Make sure you consider what you plan to wear. Choose your outfit carefully. There are many different styles for different types of jobs. Here are some quick tips that make sense for most situations:

- **Don't wear jeans, tank tops, shorts, or other very casual clothes.** Even if it looks good on you, it isn't good in an interview. If you doubt your choices, then ask someone for their opinion or don't wear it.

- **Be conservative.** Interviews are not a place to be trendy and hip.

    If your goal is to remain unemployed, and you're on your way to a job interview wearing any of the below, congratulations! You can look forward to the deafening silence of prospective employers not returning your calls.

- **Anything you would wear to a bar.**

    If the see-through top you wore last night got you free drinks, it'll get you a job, right? Riiiiight…uh, wrong. Whether you're flashing cleavage or chest hair, button up your shirt and keep your undies a secret.

- **Look-at-me colors or patterns.** Hot pink, lime green and hooker red are all on the top ten list of colors employers love not to see in their office. Fussy prints or bold retro patterns are equally obnoxious. When it comes to interviews, black is the new black.

- **Shoes you've worn only once…or too often.**

    What's the most unprofessional: staggering across the room on 3-inch heels you didn't practice walking in, or leaving a trail of dust on the company carpet? Shoes tell a prospective employer everything they need to know about your attention to detail.

- **Anything that tells a prospective employer you're a pet owner.**

    The realization that you own a white poodle who loves to snuggle up against your black blazer is rarely followed by, "You're hired!" Check and double-check for drool, fur or paw prints before you make your entrance.

- **Cologne, aftershave, makeup, jewelry.**

Don't use too much cologne or aftershave; you don't want to walk into an interview smelling like a perfume factory. What if your interviewer is allergic to perfume or cologne? That is a possibility. You don't want them going into an allergic reaction and not be able to interview you. Or maybe remind them of someone they don't like.

Keep the jewelry to a minimum. No real dangly earrings, big thick necklaces, etc. You don't want to wear things that could be distracting.

Makeup. Your makeup should be natural and not look like you are going out to paint the town! Have a makeover at one of the makeup counters in a department store. They are free and you might get some great tips.

Now you know what not to wear, there's no excuse for an interview faux pas—at least where your outfit's concerned. And for those who think clothes are less important than qualifications, consider this: you're competing against dozens of equally qualified candidates for the same position. Can you afford to be the one who makes a tasteless first impression?

Prepare for the Ten most Frequently Asked Interview Questions

There are as many different possible interview questions as there are interviewers, so being prepared to answer the most common questions can be helpful. If you are targeting positions that are a good fit, answering questions during the interview should not be too difficult if the postion is in line with your skills and experiences.

1. Tell me about yourself.
2. What are your strengths?
3. What are your weaknesses?
4. Why should I hire you?
5. What sor of compensation do you expect?
6. How does your experience relate to the job we have open?
7. Where would you like to be in your career five years from now?
8. What would your former employers (or references) say about you?
9. Why are you looking for this type of position and why here?
10. Tell me why you left your last position.

Research the Company

By learning all you can about the company ahead of time, it will be to your advantage and help make a great impression in your interview. So, for example, if you know the company is expanding you can emphasize your skills that can help make that expansion more successful. Or perhaps you find out that the interviewer has a particular hobby, you can use it to break the ice at the beginning of the interview. You can go to your local library and have one of the librarians assist you in getting information form on-line databases, news stories, and other information resources.

Considering the following points when doing your research:

- **The organization**
    - Company size, number of employees
    - Major product or services
    - Competitors and the competitive environment
    - Major changes in policies or status
    - Reputation, values
    - Major weaknesses or opportunities
- **The Interviewer**
    - Level and area or responsibility
    - Special projects, interests and accomplishments
    - Personal information (family, hobbies, and so on)
    - Management style
- **The position**
    - Does an opening or similar job exist now?
    - What happened to others in the position or similar positions?
    - What is the salary range and benefits?
    - Duties and responsibilities

Prepare some questions. In addition to answering honestly and well to an interviewer's questions, asking questions of your own at the end of an interview will further demonstrate your interest in the position. Do some research on the company and jot down about 4-5 questions in advance.

QUESTIONS TO ASK AN INTERVIEWER

At the end of a typical interview the interviewer will usually ask if you have any questions. You should be prepared, however, to ask questions throughout the entire interview to demonstrate your interest in the position and to ensure the interview is a dialogue rather than a monologue.

By cleverly placing relevant questions within your interview discussion, you can subtly validate your knowledge of the company, the industry, and your long-term interest with that organization. At the same time, do not flood the screener with a lot of questions because it will look as if you are conducting a cross-examination. Two or three thoughtful questions are usually adequate.

One of the purposes of the questions is clearly to gain information from the interviewer. Good questions, however, can make a very positive impression by displaying that you are comprehensive, interested, sharp, and experienced. Adapt and communicate these questions to your particular functional level (entry, mid management, senior executive) and industry.

For examples of great questions visit: The Interview Question Database provide at http://www.quintcareers.com/interview_question_database:

There you will find 150 typical traditional and behavioral job interview questions that employers ask of job seekers for both established job seekers and college students and recent graduates.

THE DAY OF THE INTERVIEW

- ✓ Get there early. Allow plenty of time to get to the interview a few minutes early. You don't want to get there too early, though, no more than 10 or 15 minutes.
- ✓ Check you appearance and other details. Before entering the interview, you should stop in a rest room and take a good look in the mirror. Make any final adjustments to your hair, clothing, etc. Get relaxed and mentally prepared to knock their socks off!
- ✓ Remember the receptionist's opinion carries a lot of weight. Make sure you are polite and professional to anyone whom you meet going in the door. I can assure you the interviewer will hear about everything you do in the waiting room.

The First Few Seconds Count

Interviewers can react to many things you say and do during the first few minutes of the interview.

- ✓ First initial greeting. Be prepared for a warm yet professional greeting. Demonstrate enthusiasm and show you are happy to be there. All though this is a business meeting, you social skills will be taken into consideration. Give a firm handshake but don't break their hand. Only give a handshake if the interviewer offers one first. Use the interviewers last name in your greeting if possible, so make sure you ask the receptionist the interviewers name in advance.
- ✓ **Posture is essential.** How you stand or sit can and will make a difference. Show interest by leaning forward in your chair when talking or listening to the interviewer. Leaning back could be viewed as being bored or uninterested.
- ✓ **Voice**. Most like you will be nervous, but try to sound friendly and enthusiastic. Make sure you don't speak too loudly or too softly and practice sounding confident.
- ✓ **Eye contact**. If you have a hard time looking people in the eye, get over it. People with poor eye contact are considered shy, insecure, and even dishonest. You don't need to stare but making eye contact while you listen or speak will make you appear more confident.
- ✓ **Distracting habits**. You might have nervous habits that you are not even aware of. Interviewers will find these annoying. A good example is if you play with your hair or clothing. Or saying something like "You know" or "Uhh" over and over again. The best way to see how others see you is to have someone video tap you in a mock interview. If that isn't possible, ask you closest friends and family to point out any habits they see that might bother an interviewer. Don't get defensive! Take constructive feedback and use it to correct your negative behaviors.
- ✓ **Allow things to happen**. Most interviews start off with an informal conversation around subjects such as the weather, sports, did you have trouble find us, and similar topics. All though this informal talk seems to have nothing to do with the interview, it does. The interviewer is trying to find out how well you relate to others socially.
- ✓ **Follow the lead**. Relax and don't feel you have to start a serious discussion off the bat. Let the interviewer lead the way.
- ✓ **Smile.** When you smile, it makes you look happy to be there and meet the interviewer.
- ✓ **Use the interviewers name in a formal way**. Use Mister or Miss unless you are asked to use another name. Say the interviewers name as often as you can in your conversation.
- ✓ **Look for things in common or use compliments**. Most offices will have photos of family or pictures of things they like. If it is a photo of kids, say nice looking family, or if it is a picture of a golf course say something about the picture.
- ✓ **Ask your prepared opening questions**. After you have spent a few minutes in a friendly conversation, you ask a question to get things rolling. Something a long the line of "Can you tell me more about your organization" or would you mind telling me? Or you could say "I have a background in _____, and I'm interested in knowing how that might fit an organization such as yours.

- ✓ **Know your key competencies**. Make sure you use the key skills you have to support the job you are interviewing for.
- ✓ **Answer problem questions**. You are bound to have an interviewer ask you a challenging question. Don't panic, be ready. If you are asked about something you have done, and you either haven't had a situation come up, or you are not sure what the interviewer is asking, be honest and don't make something up. You can ask the interviewer, for example, or you can say; you haven't had that kind of situation in your past positions. The interviewer will ask something else! Try to speak at least 20 seconds but not more than about two minutes when answer questions. You don't want to ramble. If you are prepared for answering questions a head of time, it will be much easier when you are actually in the real interview. Practice does make perfect.
- ✓ **Know something about the job**. Look up the description if you haven't been given one. You can find job descriptions in the Occupational Handbook available on line or at the library. You can also do an Internet search for the description. Then you can emphasize why are the best person to do the job well.
- ✓ **Have supportive documents**. Make sure you take extra copies of your resume, letters of reference and reference list. If you use the "Active Interview" method, take several copies of your presentation.
- ✓ **Give the employer a reason to hire you over your competitors**. If you want the job, think about it a head of time and give the employer at least one or more great reasons why you should be hired.
- ✓ **Ask if there is anything else you can provide**. This can include, a portfolio, transcripts, background information or more. You want your interviewer to have all the information he or she needs, and actively offering it strengthens your enthusiasm for the job.
- ✓ **Summarize and restate your interest and enthusiasm for the position**. You want the interviewer to feel you strongly desire the position. If, for some reason, any problems, or weaknesses come up, reassure they will not keep you from doing an excellent job.
- ✓ **If you want the job ask for it**. Often employers will hire someone based on the fact they asked for the job, and you have demonstrated your skills, enthusiasm and genuine interest in the company. A good question to consider. "Tell me what I would need to do in the first 90 days of being in the position for you to say I was the best candidate you ever hired? This will take them by surprise, and they will give you some things they expect. You can always include a summary of how you will do this in your follow up thank your letter!
- ✓ **Use the callback technique**. All though it is uncomfortable sometimes to use this technique and can be to your advantage. Here is what you should do:
    - o Thank the interviewer by name
    - o Express your sincere interest in the job and the company

- Arrange a reason and time to contact the employer again
- Say good-bye

Example:

While shaking hands with the interviewer, say "Thank you so much, Mr. Smith, for all your time today."

Tell the employer: "The position we talked about today is a perfect fit and exactly what I have been looking for. I am so impressed by your organization, and I am confident I can make a great contribution to your team.

Reason and time to call back: If the interviewer has been helpful and impressed with you, he or she won't mind if you follow up. It's important to arrange a day and time to contact the employer again. Don't expect them to contact you. Say something like "I'm sure other questions will come to mind. When would it be the best time to get back to you?"

Say goodbye: After setting the day and time, again say thanks by using their name and say goodbye.

AFTER THE INTERVIEW

- ✓ Send a thank-you note. Within 24, hours or sooner, make sure you send a thank you note. You can do this either by mail or email, if you want. If you interviewed with more than one person, send a separate note to each person and don't say the exact same thing. Highlight something each person said and talk about that.
- ✓ Follow up as promised. If you said you would call at a certain time, make sure you do. This will certainly impress the interviewer and show that you are organized and follow through with commitments.

Even if you are not interested in pursuing the position it is still important to follow up. You never know what the future holds or whom they might know. One day you may need to reach out to this recruiter or hiring manager again in the future.

Thank You Note After Interview

ROBERT SMITH
1234 South Lake Drive, Any town, Any State 34567
(555) 567-8900 • Email: jobsearcher@aol.com

Mr. John Doe   (insert date)
Partner
Doe, Smith, Kennedy, Sampson & Patterson
3355 Main Street
Any town, Any State 30337

Dear Mr. Doe:

I want to thank you for meeting with me on August 23, 20XX. I am very excited about the potential opportunities we discussed and believe that they are an excellent fit for my career goals. In particular, there are various areas you mentioned that would utilize my experience.

1. Building your intellectual property practice so that it embraces the spectrum of intellectual property matters including patents, trademarks and unfair competition, copyrights, trade secrets, licensing and litigation in these areas. As mentioned during our discussion, for the past fifteen years my work as an attorney has been primarily focused in the business advisory role, including licensing and strategic planning of patenting of intellectual property for various technologies.

2. Identifying the specialized areas within a patent practice group, and the potential clients desiring to obtain outside counsel. Those patent practice areas typically include chemistry/chemical engineering, mechanical engineering, electrical engineering and computer practice and biotechnology. For the past eleven years, I have been involved in the preparation and prosecution of patent applications in the chemical and pharmaceutical technology in both the domestic and foreign markets.

Additionally, I have prepared and filed trademark and copyright applications. My prior experience in the government, corporate, and private sectors have provided me with a unique opportunity to participate in the patent process from various perspectives. This, I believe could be a benefit to your firm as the intellectual property area is constantly changing.

Of course, other areas such as the logistics of supporting intellectual property would also have to be taken into consideration when building an intellectual property practice. During my practice in the intellectual property area, I have worked closely with the support staff (administrative, paralegal, docketing, etc.) to assure that all documents are in compliance with mandated formalities and are timely filed in each country that protection is sought.

Once again, Mr. Doe, thank you for your interest in my career. I look forward to speaking with you again in the near future to discuss further details of the potential working relationship we can establish.

Sincerely,

Robert S. Smith

Following up appropriately can make the difference between hearing *You're hired!* Or getting the rejection letter in the mail, if you are lucky to even get one.

SALARY RESEARCH

Geographical preference, economic trends locally, regionally and nationally, and market demand play an important role in determining a fair salary / compensation. The best sources of salary market intelligence are often times through trade associations and networking with national and local chapter leaders to identify best salary range.

Salaries can vary greatly due to company, location, industry, experience and benefits. Also, salaries during a deep recession usually reflect organizational stagnation, moratoriums on salary increases, or other events that can cause wide fluctuations in salary intelligence. Best source to get localized salary market intelligence is to check with your local Chamber of Commerce, industry trade associations including blogs or forums on www.LinkedIn.com, local chapter trade associations (speak to President or Vice President of that organization).

For additional salary information, we recommend visiting:

www.payscale.com	www.vault.com
www.salaryexpert.com	www.glassdoor.com
www.salary.com	http://jobstar.org/tools/salary/sal-prof.php
http://www.rileyguide.com/execpay.html	www.homefair.com

QUICK TIPS FOR NEGOTIATING JOB AND SALARY OFFERS

1. Always Avoid Initial Discussion Of Salary. Use the strategic negotiations techniques and remember, whoever discusses salary first is at a disadvantage in the negotiation.

    - Generally, most job searchers are offered a salary that is near the mid-point of the range that is budgeted for the position. It would be very unusual for the interviewer to make the initial offer much beyond the midpoint. After a company has presented the base salary offer, they will discuss other benefits. This is not the time to negotiate.

    - Keep in mind that your next position may be a bridge job that leads to even greater opportunities and that your optimum compensation package may be deferred until you have crossed that bridge.

2. Ask questions as to what they are offering as well as on areas that they may not have presented, such as vacation policy or severance issues. During this initial presentation, do not display too much emotion (don't appear desperate), but merely gather information.

3. Once the offer has been extended and all the benefits have been discussed, do not accept or reject it at that time. Politely tell the company that you will need a few days to review the entire compensation package. Then, schedule a meeting with me for review and to brainstorm the strategy. I will recommend a strategy for your counter offer.

INTERNET CAREER RESOURCES

With the development of the Internet, has come a huge collection of job search resources for job seekers of all kinds. Here are some sites to get you started. There are thousands resources on the internet.

DICTIONARY AND LANGUAGE RESOURCES

- 11 Rules of Writing – www.junketstudies.com/joomla/11-rules-of-writing/the-rules: This site is a concise guide to some of the most commonly violated rules of writing.
- Acronym Finder – www.acronym.com: With more than 900,000 human-edited definitions, Acronym Finder is the world's largest and most comprehensive dictionary of acronyms, abbreviations, and initialisms.
- Advice on Research and Writing - www.cs.cmu.edu/afs/cs.cmu.edu/user/mleone/web/how-to.html: A collection of advice about how to do research and how to communicate effectively (primarily for computer scientists).
- Allwords.com - English dictionary with multi-lingual search.
- Barkley's Financial Glossary - www.oasismanagement.com/glossary/
- Cambridge Dictionaries Online – www.cambridge.dictionary.org: An online search engine allowing users to find definitions.
- DOD Dictionary of Military Terms - www.dtic.mil/doctrine/dod_dictionary/DOD: Dictionary of Military and Associated Terms.
- Dictionary.com - "Dictionary.com - the largest and most trusted free online dictionary. Quickly find accurate definitions and audio pronunciations of words."
- Dictionary of Difficult Words - www.talktalk.co.uk/reference/dictionaries/difficultwords   index of over 13,900 difficult words from The Hutchinson Dictionary of Difficult Words. Use as a resource for increasing your vocabulary, for word games and puzzles, or just for enjoying and enriching your word power.
- DOT - Dictionary of Occupational Titles - www.wave.net/upg/immigration/dot_index.htmlIt's: the official dictionary of occupational titles. DOT's database is arranged alphabetically and can be read online or downloaded in one file.
- Duhaime's Law Dictionary - www.duhaime.org/LegalDictionary: Researched, written in plain language and provided free of charge, to the WWLIA and its users, by lawyer Lloyd Duhaime.

- English Grammar - www.englishgrammar.org/: "Download English grammar rules review, English grammar lessons and grammar exercises for free, or get grammar help and ESL tips on proper grammar usage."
- Free Online Spell Checker - www.spellcheckonline.com/: "This free online spell checker and spell check enables you to check your texts for spelling, grammar, or punctuation mistakes and offers instant feedback to correct spelling errors."
- FreeTranslation.com - www.freetranslation.com/: "FreeTranslation.com is a straight forward, easy-to-use site for rapid translations where you can get the 'gist' of foreign language text and web pages."
- Glossary of Business Terms: Washington Post - www.washingtonpost.com/wp-dyn/business/specials/glossary/index.html
- Glossary of Stock Market Terms: Nasdaq - www.nasdaq.com/investing/glossary/
- Glossary of Wireless Terms - www.wirelessadvisor.com/resources/glossary
- Grammar and Style Notes – www.andromeda.rutgers.edu/~jlynch/Writing/: by Jack Lynch
- GrammarCheck.net - "Now you can grammar and spell check any text or document online. Simply copy and paste your text onto our website to proofread, review, and correct it."
- subject-verb agreement and the use of articles to exercises in parallel structures and help with argumentative essays, and a way to submit questions about grammar and writing."
- Legal Dictionary: FindLaw - http://dictionary.findlaw.com/
- TechTerms.com contains hundreds of computer and technology terms, all with detailed explanations."
- Vocabulary.com: Dictionary - "Try the world's fastest, smartest dictionary: Start typing a word and you'll see the definition. Unlike most online dictionaries, we want you to find your word's meaning quickly. We don't care how many ads you see or how many pages you view. In fact, most of the time you'll find the word you are looking for after typing only one or two letters."

JOB BOARDS

- After College -- a job and internship site for college students and recent college grads. Post your resume or search for job openings (by job type, industry, type of work, location, and keyword). Also includes some basic career resources. Free to jobseekers.
- Best Jobs in the USA Today -- a comprehensive job resource site that includes jobs databases, corporate profiles, resume posting, and a career resources store.
- BilingualCareer.com -- where bilingual job-seekers (English and at least one other language) can search job listings (by language, location, industry, keywords), post your resume, and find job interviewing and resume preparation advice. Free to job-seekers.

- CareerBuilder -- claims to have the largest assortment of job listings on the Net -- a combination of help wanted ads of the nation's leading newspapers and job listings from the Web sites of leading employers. The site also includes many other resources. Free to job-seekers.
- Careercast -- a cool job portal offering job-seekers opportunities from all U.S. and Canadian newspaper, magazine, niche and TV station Websites powered by Adicio Inc., a developer of Web-based classified advertising solutions. Job-seekers can search job listings (by keyword, category, location), post a resume, find job news, more. No cost to job-seekers.
- CareerPark.com -- where job-seekers can search or browse job postings, as well as post your resume. Include links to other key career and job sites. Free to job-seekers.
- College Recruiter -- Jobs for college students, grads and recent graduates. Entry-level work and career opportunities. Part-time and full-time. A great resource for job-seekers.
- CareerSonar.com--Discover the best career opportunities hidden in your social and professional networks.
- Dice.com -- a great job site for technology professionals. Job-seekers can search through thousands of job openings (by job type, location, as well as by metro area or employer), post your resume and confidential profile, create an email job alert, and find great career resources. Free to job-seekers
- DiversityWorking.com -- a great diversity job site for all ethnic and sexual orientation groups, where job-seekers can search for jobs (by location, industry, job listing type, posting recency,
- and keywords), as well as post your resume, and sign up for a free newsletter. The company is also a national career expo producer for the diversity marketplace. Free to job-seekers.
- EmploymentGuide.com -- a great resource for job-seekers, where you can search for jobs, post your resume, and find career advice. One of the site's greatest resources is the development of localized job sites (a total of 56 metropolitan areas) so that job-seekers looking for employment in a specific geographic area can find the best job listings. Free to job-seekers
- Employment911.com -- a "one-stop" job site, where job-seekers can search more than 350 major job sites with more than 3 million job openings and create an online resume that is posted to thousands of employers. Also includes some great career articles, tools, links, free email accounts, and much more. Free to job-seekers.
- FindARecruiter.com -- where job-seekers who are looking for a recruiting professional (headhunters, executive search, staffing firms) can search a database of more than 10,000 recruiters. Search by company name, specialty, or location. Free to job-seekers.
- FreshJobs.com -- where all job postings are no older than one week. Job-seekers can search for jobs by location, skills, benefits, job type, or company as well as post your resume. You can also get a confidential mailbox and sign-up for a job matching service. Free to job-seekers.

- GetTheJob.com -- a job search engine for direct employer jobs only, collecting job postings from the corporate career centers of thousands of companies, indexing more than 2 million jobs at any time. Job-seekers can search job postings, register for email alerts. No cost to job-seekers.
- GOJobs.com -- a general job board where job-seekers can search job postings by keyword or browse by state or job function. You can also create an email job agent as well as find some career resources. Free to job-seekers.
- Indeed.com -- a meta-search job site that pulls job postings from more than 500 places, including the major job boards, the top 200 newspapers, hundreds of professional associations, and company career centers. Job-seekers can search for job listings by (what: title, keywords, company; and where: location). No cost to job-seekers.
- The Interview Exchange -- a new concept in job boards, where job-seekers who are interested in job listings are rated based on how closely you match the qualifications in the job posting. Job-seekers can also post your resume and receive e-mail job matching notification. Free to job-seekers.
- jobalot.com -- a mega-meta job site, where job-seekers can use a simple job search interface (searching basically by keywords and location) to find thousands of the job listings from hundreds of the best job sites. You can also browse jobs by category, find career resources, or learn about continuing education opportunities. No cost to job-seekers.
- JobCircle.com -- Mid-Atlantic's largest non-newspaper affiliated job board that provides
- careers, content and community to jobseekers -- operating in CT, DC, DE, OH, MD, NY, NJ, PA, VA and WV. Job-seekers can search or browse job listings, as well as post your resume. No cost to job-seekers.
- Jobfox -- a job-matching site for job-seekers, which uses its *Mutual Suitability System* -- an in-depth profile system used to learn about your experience, wants, and needs -- to then present you with only the opportunities (rated on a 5-star scale) that match your profile. (Employers participate in this same process.) No cost to job-seekers for basic services.
- Jobirn: Insider Referral Network -- a unique job site that is a combination of job board, online interview system, and employee referral system that connects job-seekers with employees inside
- the company where you would like to work -- to help get a referral to ideal job. No cost to job-seekers.
- Job Search Shortcuts -- a great job-search site that provides links directly to more than 20,000 company career centers job listing Web pages in 41 metropolitan areas nationwide. Jobs are categorized both by city within each metro area as well as alphabetically -- and links send job-seekers directly to the employer. No cost to job-seekers.
- JobShouts! -- a job search engine integrated with social media, helping to create connections and deliver better matching results for job seekers, which delivers real-time job postings and automated one click searching across multiple social networks simultaneously. No cost to jobseekers.

- Jobs in Pods -- a Web 2.0 job site in which job-seekers can listen to employer "jobcasts" -- audio interviews from employer HR managers/employees that discuss corporate culture, benefits, etc. At the end of each podcast you're instructed on how and where to apply to the jobs you just heard about. Each podcast also comes with a blog post, which lists all the relevant links and information about the employer and job listings. No cost to job-seekers.
- Jobs.NET -- job-seekers from all over the world can browse or search for jobs, post your confidential online resume, and receive job-hunting tips and advice. Job posting can be searched by just about any criteria, including keywords, location, regency of posting, salary, job title, industry, company size, and more. Free to job-seekers.
- JobsINBOX -- an international job search engine and networking site, where job-seekers can find relevant job postings from around the world through a matching process based on key skills. You can also create communities of your work interest, offer/receive advice/info/help from others with the same interests. No cost to job-seekers.
- Jobzerk -- a self-proclaimed world's first community and socially-driven job site, where job-seekers can easily interact with other members and publish useful information about themselves, the job search, or hiring process. No cost to job-seekers.
- Juju -- an interesting resource -- one of the best, where job-seekers can search 15 different job sites (including CareerCity, CareerMosaic, HeadHunter.net, JobOptions, NationJob, and others) using keywords that describe your preferred job, as well as a preferred location. Free.
- LatPro -- the worldwide leader in online employment for Hispanic and bilingual professionals, where job-seekers can search thousands of job listings from pre-screened employers, post multiple resume versions, create an email job agent, and access other career resources. Free to job-seekers.
- LinkUp -- a job search engine that only lists jobs taken directly from more than 20,000 legitimate company Websites. The site claims it only shows current openings; listings are removed if a company removes the posting from its Website. Job-seekers can search job listings (by keyword, location) and apply directly to the employer. No cost to job-seekers.
- LocalHelpWanted.net -- lots of features and benefits to this job site where job-seekers can search for job listings by first narrowing choices by state and major city. You can also post your resume, audio resume, video resume, and portfolio items after registration. For an additional fee, you can obtain addition space to post even more information. No cost to job-seekers for basic services.
- Monster.com -- one of the oldest job sites on the Web, with several hundred thousand jobs worldwide. Also includes career advice and relocation services for job-seekers, as well as an auction-style marketplace for independent professionals.
- myCareerSpace -- where job-seekers can search for jobs (by category, region, or keywords) and post up to five different resumes that you can then use to apply to job openings online. Also includes

other job-seeker resources, such as career expos, relocation, insurance, and more. Free to job-seekers.

- NationJob Network -- an online job search service with thousands of current job listings and company profiles. Includes an email service that send you jobs that match your qualifications and interests.
- Net-Temps -- a site where job-seekers can search thousands of job listings or post your resume. Includes contract, temporary and permanent employment postings. Also includes career development articles, tools and resources. A top site. Free to job-seekers.
- Realmatch.com -- takes the job-seeker's qualifications and preferences and matches them with the employer's requirements. You can also search job listings by keyword and location. Free to job-seekers
- Simply Hired -- a job search engine where job-seekers can search job listings by keyword and get results from a multitude of sources. Also offers you the opportunity to get updates when new jobs are posted -- by email, social networks, blogs, your homepage, and even your mobile phone. Free to job-seekers.
- SnagAJob.com -- largest job site for part-time and full-time hourly jobs. Job-seekers can search for a job by type of job or by location, as well as register for email alerts. Also includes career resources and advice. Free to job-seekers.
- thingamajob.com -- a free career site for all job seekers from the Allegis Group. Job searches, online resume posting, job alerts, and career tools, are a few of the many features available to job-seekers. You can search for jobs by job categories, keywords, location, and date the job was posted. Free to job-seekers.
- TopUSAJobs.com -- a job site that lists the top jobs from numerous "niche" industry and geographic-specific job boards. Job-seekers can search for job listings (by category, location, job title, and job detail keywords), or go directly to the individual job boards. Free to job-seekers.
- TweetMyJobs -- with 8,000+ vertical job channels segmented by geography, job type, and industry, this site is able to connect employers and recruiters with job-seekers instantly any time a new job is posted. Simple register to get instant notification of newly posted job opportunities and internships. No cost to job-seekers.
- TwitterJobSearch.com -- a job search engine for Twitter, where job-seekers enter search keyword(s) and receive immediate results of tweets for job openings. No cost to job-seekers.
- USAJOBS -- a one-stop source for job-seekers seeking information about jobs and employment with the United States Federal Government. Job-seekers can search for jobs (by keyword, location, and occupation), post your resume, and register for a job-matching email service. Also includes lots of other resources and tips for finding employment with the government. Free to job-seekers.

- US.jobs -- a national employment network formed by an alliance between two nonprofit associations to provide job seekers in all industries and occupations, entry-level to chief executive officer, employment and career opportunities nationwide. Search postings or browse by company. No cost to job-seekers.
- Vault.com -- well-known for its insider reports on thousands of companies, this site has branched out into recruitment and has more than 150,000 job postings from about 27,000 employers, which job-seekers can search through multiple criteria (such as job categories, keywords, location, experience level, posting date). Job-seekers can also sign-up for an email job criteria matching service. Free to job-seekers.
- VetJobs.com -- a great site for veterans and transitioning military personnel and their family members. Job openings for all levels and types of jobs. You can search for jobs (by type, keyword, and location), as well as post your resume. Includes other key resources for vets. Sponsored by Veterans of Foreign Wars of the United States. Free to jobseekers.

COMPANY RESEARCH PORTALS

www.google.com/Top/Business/	www.smartbrief.com
www.linkedIn.com and other social media	http://findarticles.com/
www.businesswire.com/	www.ZoomInfo.com
http://biz.yahoo.com/ic/ (Yahoo Finance!)	www.555-1212.com
www.hoovers.com (Hoover's Business Profiles)	http://www.forbes.com/lists/
www.bizjournals.com/	www.referenceusa.com

ADDITIONAL SITES THAT YOU WILL FIND HELPFUL

Glassdoor - www.glassdoor.com - a popular site for inside information on what it's *really* like to work for companies, plus salary information. Glassdoor also has a LinkedIn Group and is a great way to stay "in the know."

Mashable – www.mashable.com is a leading source for news, information & resources **for the Connected Generation.** Mashable reports on the importance of digital innovation and how it empowers and inspires people around the world. Mashable's 20 million monthly unique visitors and 6 million social media followers have become one of the most engaged online news communities.

Free Business Cards - www.vistaprint.com

Business cards are an essential tool for the job seeker. You will be astonished at the chances you will have to pass them out. When you meet people at networking events, you will want to have cards to exchange.

Business cards are a way for people to recall you, remember the type of job opportunities to refer to you, and have your contact information to include you in their network. The information you put on your cards should include at least Your Name, Email Address, Title Of The Type Of Position You Are Targeting, Linkedin Profile Link, City, State and Phone Number(s).

To maximize your value you might want to include a few of your strengths, certifications, or relevant skills. For example, if you are a computer programmer, you might want to include the languages in which you program. Keep the information brief and relevant. Don't forget to take advantage of the space on the back of the card (shipping charges will apply).

JibberJobber - www.jibberjobber.com by Jason Alba: Allows you to keep track of the information you collect during a job search. Track the companies that you apply to (Target Companies). Track each job that you apply for and log the status of each application (date of first interview, date thank you letter sent, etc.). Want to know where you sent your different resumes? Use JibberJobber to keep track of it!

iBest Presentations - www.interviewbest.com, by Eric Kramer. This will be a resource you will definitely want to explore. Because the interview process in broken, job seekers must be in control of the interview process. This will set you miles apart in your next interview. iBest is an innovative, online presentation preparation process that prepares job seekers and candidates for their next interview. Interview presentations have been used in hundreds of interviews.

For more great resources on job boards and associations check out:
http://www.weddles.com/booksforjobseekers.cfm

WEDDLE's Guide to Employment Sites on the Internet

Called the Zagat of the online employment services industry, this print guide includes WEDDLE's choice for The Top 100, those sites that are among the elite of the online employment services industry, and The Best & the Rest, a directory of over 9,000 sites - the largest available anywhere - organized by career field, industry and other factors

WEDDLE's Guide to Association Web Sites

This one-of-a-kind guide provides a listing of the online employment resources - the job board, resume database, online networking capability - available at over 3,000 professional societies and trade associations organized by career field, industry and other factors.

CAN CAREER COACHING SERVICES BENEFIT MY CAREER?

One of the most recent developments in the job search industry is the evolution of the career coach as an essential component for any top-level job search campaign. We hear about coaches in the media, read about them in resume books, and even see them on Oprah! Five years ago, coaching was a virtually unknown profession. Today, it is evolving at a phenomenal rate.

Are you taking advantage of this new trend? Do you know what a career coach is? Could you benefit from the expertise of one?

By definition, a career coach is a trained professional (usually someone in the counseling and/or professional job search industry) who will guide you through the complexities of skills assessments, job search planning, campaign development, career marketing and long-term career management. To determine the value a career coach would bring to you, go through the following checklist of information.

Career Assessment & Focus

Yes	No	
☐	☐	Do you know "who" you are – professionally?
☐	☐	Do you have a clear understanding of your most significant skills and qualifications?
☐	☐	Are you clear about your career objectives?
☐	☐	Do your skills and qualifications match your objectives?
☐	☐	Do you know the type of position you are seeking?
☐	☐	Do you know what types of activities you do NOT want to engage in?
☐	☐	Do you know the industries in which you are interested and will be focusing your search?

Your career coach will assist you in identifying and assessing your qualifications, job preferences, likes/dislikes, immediate objectives and long-term goals, and they will help you evaluate your worth in the employment market and your value within specific industries.

Career Change & Transition

Yes	No	
☐	☐	Are you considering changing career paths, professions, or industries?
☐	☐	Can you find an equivalent position if you make such a change?
☐	☐	Will you command the same level of compensation?
☐	☐	What skills do you have that are transferable between jobs and/or industries?
☐	☐	Do you feel as though you are going to be niched into your current industry for the rest of your career?
☐	☐	Do you feel as though you are going to be niched into your current profession for the rest of your career?
☐	☐	Do you know today's "hot" industries and professions?
☐	☐	Do you have the "right" skills to transition into these high-growth industries?

Your coach will guide you in identifying and evaluating all of your possibilities and provide you with critical market intelligence to formulate your job search action plan.

Personal & Family Issues

Yes	No	
☐	☐	Do you have personal or family issues that are directly impacting your job search?
☐	☐	Is relocation out of the question?
☐	☐	Is your spouse currently employed and not anxious to leave his/her position?
☐	☐	Is your age impacting your campaign results?

Yes	No	
☐	☐	Are you tied to your current community because of out-of-work activities you're involved in?
☐	☐	Do you have a physical disability that might be negatively impacting your search, but has never impacted your work performance?
☐	☐	Are you depressed because your job search has not progressed at the pace you anticipated?
☐	☐	Do you need an advisor, a confidante, or a job search partner?

Your coach can be your sounding board, helping you determine how to evaluate and prioritize these issues in relation to your search, how to best overcome obstacles standing in your way, and how to best position those issues to your advantage.

Career Marketing & Job Search Management

Yes	No	
☐	☐	Do you understand that the job search process is similar to the sales process?
☐	☐	Do you understand that YOU are the product you are selling and that you must effectively merchandise and promote the product?
☐	☐	Do you understand all of the different marketing channels available to you in managing your search – targeted direct mail campaigns, email broadcast campaigns, Internet resume posting services, Internet job posting services, specialty job lead reports and more?
☐	☐	Do you know which marketing channels are the RIGHT marketing channels for your search?
☐	☐	Do you know how to best optimize your networking contacts and results?
☐	☐	Do you know which advertisements to respond to and which to ignore?

Your career coach can help you critically evaluate each and every available job search strategy, its value to your search, the risk/reward ratio of each, and how to best integrate each program into your campaign.

Interview Skills & Salary Negotiations

Yes	No	
☐	☐	Are you confident of your performance in the interview situation?
☐	☐	Are you able to "sell" your accomplishments without sounding as though you are bragging?
☐	☐	Are you articulate and well presented?
☐	☐	Are you comfortable in a "stressful" interviewing situation with more than one interviewer?
☐	☐	Can you quickly and easily accommodate to a new environment?
☐	☐	Are you an accomplished negotiator, confident of your ability to negotiate the "best" compensation package possible?
☐	☐	Do you fully understand the potential of various bonus structures and schedules?
☐	☐	Do you understand the value of equity participation and other non-traditional compensation models?

Your career coach will help you develop and refine powerful interviewing skills, pushing you to perform at your best, communicate your value and earn a compensation package well beyond your original expectations.

References

Yes	No	
☐	☐	Will your references speak positively about your skills, qualifications, experience and track record?
☐	☐	Will your references say anything that could be potentially damaging to you?
☐	☐	Are your references the RIGHT references for you to use?
☐	☐	Do you know how to improve the performance of your references when they're talking about you?
☐	☐	Can you make the reference-checking process easier for your references?

If you know that your references may be divulging information that could be construed as negative, let your career coach teach you how to best overcome these situations.

If you can answer, "YES" to most of the questions and are confident in your ability to manage your job search, then you are reasonably well prepared to move forward on your own. However, if you still feel the need for the expertise, insights, and support of a career coach, don't hesitate for one minute. These trained professionals can make a huge difference in the speed and success of your job search.

If you answered "NO" to more than just 3-4 of the questions above, I would strongly urge you to consider the value a career coach could bring to your job search, career performance, and compensation. With years of training and experience, career coaches know what works and what doesn't work, how to optimize your results, and how to help you land your ideal position. With your career coach at your side, you can move forward confidently and successfully.

ABOUT THE COMMUNITY JOB CLUB, INC.
WHERE WE STARTED AND WHO WE ARE TODAY

The Community Job Club, Inc. is a 501(c) 3 organization that offers free or low cost job-search training organization for experienced professionals of all ages who are actively seeking better career opportunities. We work with job seekers from new grads to seasoned professionals or anyone interested in shaping up their job search for faster results. Community Job Club, Inc. offers training classes, advice from professional speakers on job-search best practices, networking opportunities, an up-to-date job-search library, and much more.

Services are available without regard to age, sex, race, or religion. We offer <u>two FREE workshops a month</u> on a variety of job-search topics in addition to networking, resume reviews, and other resources to assist job seekers in organizing their job search. Other services are available and are provided on a sliding-fee scale to ensure that the programs and services provided by the Community

Job Club, Inc. are accessible to everyone who attends our programs. You will meet and hear outstanding speakers address a wide range of topics relevant to your career transition.

Although many communities provide some type of services for job seekers, we believe the Community Job Club, Inc. is unique due to the dedication of our founder and Executive Director, Diana Miller. Diana has created a model for job clubs that has been recognized by the U.S. Department of Labor Faith-Based and Neighborhood Partnerships Office as a promising practice and is becoming the "go-to" club for those wanting to start a job club in their community.

History of the Community Job Club

In 2009, the job club had its start at Mocha Joe's Coffee Shop in Stow, Ohio. Current Executive Director, Diana Miller, had gone through a career transition herself and was inspired to start the club after visiting job clubs in nearby communities. Her goal was to help those in Stow/Munroe Falls area and surrounding communities make the job search a little less lonely. "<u>Hearing the stories of those in transition, who at no fault of their own have lost their jobs, was heartbreaking,</u>" Miller said.

In 2010, after several meetings in the Coffee Shop, it was determined that the space was no longer adequate to meet the needs of the club. At this time the Stow Clergy Association was contacted for support. The Stow United Church of Christ offered assistance and the space for the job club beginning in April 2010.

In 2010, the name "Community Job Club" became the official name of the group, the domain name was purchased, and the communityjobclub.com website was built. In 2011, Diana received a call from the U.S.

Department of Labor Faith-Based and Neighborhood Partnerships Office and was asked to be part of an initiative they were working on called *Partnerships Community of Practice* - an online meeting spot to connect job clubs nationwide. You can visit this site at www.dol.gov/jobclubs. There you will find best practices, tools and resources to help facilitate partnerships with other job clubs and One-Stop Career Centers funded by the department through the Workforce Investment Act.

In 2011, Diana was also invited to participate in a round-table discussion led by Secretary of Labor Hilda L. Solis during a live webcast along with job club leaders from around the country. Diana has had the honor of being invited to the White House on two occasions to participate in other initiatives sponsored by both the White House Faith-Based and Neighborhood Partnerships Office and U.S. Department of Labor's Center for Faith-Based and Neighborhood Partnerships Office.

In September 2011, Diana was invited to the grand opening activities of the Brevard Workforce Center in Rockledge, Florida. The event included NASA leaders and other VIPs from around the country including Alicia Kelly, Director of the White House Center for Faith-Based and Neighborhood 28 Partnerships Office. Diana was one of the keynote presenters to more than 50 faith-based and other community leaders from the area.

Diana has been involved with other job club events sponsored by the U.S. Department of Labor including one in Cleveland, Ohio where she served as a moderator for a panel on area job clubs. Ben Siegel, Deputy Director of the U.S. Department of Labor's Center for Faith-Based and Neighborhood Partnerships Office, made a quick trip to Stow after the Cleveland event to have a cup of coffee at Mocha Joe's, where it all began. Sara Drew, currently Stow's mayor, and Pastor Jim Case, from the Stow Community United Church of Christ, joined in to share their support.

In September 2011, the job club filed to become a non-profit organization with hopes of expanding services to offer more support for job seekers and their families. Once again, space became an issue with the need to be open more hours and offer expanded programming.

At this time Diana reached out to Mike Weddle, the Director of Development for the City of Stow. He was very supportive of the CJC mission and became one of the club's greatest advocates. Mike arranged a meeting with Sharlene and Mark Chesnes, the owners of Stratford Place, to discuss the possibility of either low cost or free space. The Chesnes', being very community-minded and generous, offered free office space and use of the training room for CJC monthly meetings. In January 2012, the CJC moved to Stratford Place where they are still located today.

As of the end of 2012, the CJC has served over 1,000 individuals from communities throughout Northeast Ohio. Many have been successful in finding employment and others continue to pursue their career search journey.

HOW TO CONNECT WITH US

Sign up for our mailing list at: www.communityjobclub.org, where you will find great tips and resources for your job search and have access to our FREE Online Career Portal! This can be accessed via our website or go to www.mycjcinc.com.

With our online career portal, our goal is to provide you with information and tools that have proven to be successful and will assist you with your job search. This site was designed after interviewing thousands of job seekers just like you!

When you complete the "Resume Wizard" you will obtain FREE advice on how to best present your credentials to potential employers along with other helpful tips. These resources are all contained within our site and the advice is "customized for you". Some of the FREE resources include:

Resume builder	Resume review
Resume cards	Sample cover letters
Job Listings from thousands of job boards	Free trade publications
Answers to difficult Interview questions	Continuing education resources
Teleconferences focused on "hot topics"	Assessment tools

2. Join our **LinkedIn** group at www.linkedin.com/groups/Community-Job-Club-Inc

3. Connect with Diana Miller on www.linkedin.com/in/dianamillercjc

4. If you need additional assistance please ask us about our individualized services based on income. You must call to make an appointment and you must provide us with your family income information in order for us to determine eligibility.

Additional Services We Offer (Sliding fee applies, based on income, can be in person or tele-coaching):

- Personalized Individual Services
- Individual Career Coaching
- Resume Tune-Ups and Resumes from Scratch

Visit our website at www.communityjobclub.org **for additional information and services**

Works Cited

Gerber, R. B. (n.d.). "The Psycology of Termination & Outplacement.

How to Get the Job You Want and the Career You Love. (n.d.). (n.d.). Retrieved from http.www.resumesystem.com

Kramer, E. *Active Interviewing.* Philadelphia, PA.

Labor, C. s. (n.d.). *CareerOneStop.* Retrieved from http://www.careeronestop.org/

Weddle, P. (n.d.). *Work Strong: Your Personal Career Fitness System.* Retrieved from http://www.careerfitness.com

Whitcomb, S. B. *Job Search Majic.*

www.ingramcontent.com/pod-product-compliance
Lightning Source LLC
Chambersburg PA
CBHW080303180526
45167CB00006B/2649